HOW TO IMPROVE YOUR SOCIAL SKILLS

WITH FOCUS ON CONVERSATION AND COMMUNICATION CONFIDENCE AND INTELLIGENCE;

ADDENDUM: KEYS TO OVERCOME ANXIETY

BRIAN JAMES

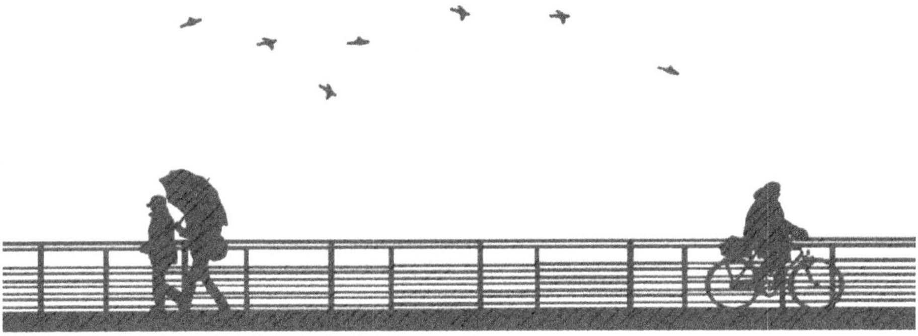

BOOK DESCRIPTION	1
INTRODUCTION	10
CHAPTER ONE	**11**
What Are Social Abilities	11
Definition of social skills	12
Types of social skills	13
Basic abilities	13
Complex skills	15
CHAPTER TWO	**23**
Why Is Good Social Skills Management So Important?	23
The importance of Social Skills	27
Importance of social skills in the company	29
Importance of Social Skills in Children	32
Importance of Social Skills in Relationships	34
CHAPTER THREE	**37**
How to Improve Social Skills	37
The Importance of Our Self-Esteem	41

How to learn social skills?	43
Helpful and Practical Advice for Improving Social Skills	48
How to Develop Your Social Skills with Body Language	51
Tips for Developing Your Child's Social Skills	55
CHAPTER FOUR	**60**
How to Behave Like a Social Person	60
Tricks to be more sociable, fun and empathetic	61
Start and end a conversation	65
CHAPTER FIVE	**68**
Verbal and Non Verbal Skills	68
Ways to Improve Your Communication Skills	71
Dealing With Awkward Silence in Conversation	74
Steps to Surviving an Awkward Conversation	78
How to start a conversation with whoever you want	82
How to communicate better with others?	85
Techniques to express yourself better and connect with other people	87

CHAPTER SIX	**90**
The Importance of Social Skills to Achieve Objectives	90
CHAPTER SEVEN	**94**
Self-Discipline	94
The importance of self-discipline.	94
How to develop self-discipline.	95
Self-Discipline to Achieve Your Goals	97
CHAPTER EIGHT	**104**
Make an excellent impression	104
CHAPTER NINE	**107**
Anxiety	107
Types of Anxiety (Characteristics, Causes, and Symptoms)	112
CHAPTER TEN	**117**
The keys to overcoming anxiety	117
Anxiety as a sign of intelligence	122
CHAPTER ELEVEN	**125**

Relaxation Techniques to Anxiety	125
CHAPTER TWELVE	**129**
Exercises to Overcome Stress and Improve Your Mental Health	129
CHAPTER THIRTEEN	**134**
Foods That Help Fight Anxiety	134
CHAPTER FOURTEEN	**139**
How anxiety affects relationships	139
Cause of Relationship Anxiety	140
Manifestations of Anxiety	142
How to End Relationship Anxiety	142
Ways to Control Relationship Anxiety	143
CHAPTER FIFTEEN	**146**
Emotional Abuse And Anxiety: How Do They Relate?	146
Emotional Abuse and Anxiety: Effects of Unseen Abuse	148
CHAPTER SIXTEEN	**150**

Anxiety at work: How the disorder interferes with working life   **150**

How does anxiety occur at work?   **150**

What are the symptoms of anxiety at work?   **152**

Consequences of anxiety at work   **153**

Prevent anxiety at work   **155**

CONCLUSION   **157**

© Copyright 2019 all rights reserved.

This document is geared towards providing exact and reliable information with regard to the topic and issue covered. The publication is sold with the idea that the publisher is not required to render accounting, officially permitted or otherwise qualified services. If advice is necessary, legal or professional, a practiced individual in the profession should be ordered.

From a Declaration of Principles which was accepted and approved equally by a Committee of the American Bar Association and a Committee of Publishers and Associations.

In no way is it legal to reproduce, duplicate, or transmit any part of this document in either electronic means or in printed format. Recording of this publication is strictly prohibited, and any storage of this document is not allowed unless with written permission from the publisher. All rights reserved.

The information provided herein is stated to be truthful and consistent, in that any liability, in terms of inattention or otherwise, by any usage or abuse of any policies, processes, or directions contained within is the solitary and utter responsibility of the recipient reader. Under no circumstances will any legal responsibility or blame be held against the publisher for any reparation, damages, or monetary loss due to the information herein, either directly or indirectly.

Respective authors own all copyrights not held by the publisher.

The information herein is offered for informational purposes solely and is universal as so.
The presentation of the information is without a contract or any type of guarantee assurance.
The trademarks that are used are without any consent, and the publication of the trademark is without permission or backing by the trademark owner. All trademarks and brands within this book are for clarifying purposes only and are owned by the owners themselves, not affiliated with this document

INTRODUCTION

How do you assess your social skills? How do you respond to criticism? Do you have a wide range of communication skills? Do you know that you can improve your social skills in many different ways?

The term 'social skills' conceals a number of important but largely learned behaviors. Improving them is just as important a task as learning to walk, read, or write. However, in many cases, we may see a dismissive approach to them or forget about these important abilities at all.

We already knew that social skills are all the necessary behaviors that allow us to interact with other people and communicate with them in an effective and satisfying way.

Below we will try to demonstrate to you some effective communication techniques that will allow you to improve your social skills. Thanks to this, you'll be able to have better relationships with people around you. And at the same time, you will learn how to solve personal conflicts quickly and efficiently.

CHAPTER ONE
What Are Social Abilities

We are social beings, so communicating with others is something that allows us to survive, grow, nurture ourselves from other points of view, and live in harmony. To do this, knowing how to relate and have a series of social skills is essential because, in most cases, we will avoid misunderstandings and conflicts.

Now, what exactly are social skills? There are those who define them as those behavioral and communication traits that make us succeed in life. However, more than success, we should talk about well-being, knowing how to live in harmony, sharing experiences, communicating effectively, and forming that social cohesion where agreements are reached, and well-being is formed that reverses directly in any aspect: the professional, personal and health.

"What really matters for success, personality, well-being, and important outcomes is a set of defined social skills, as well as cognitive skills measured by traditional IQ tests."

-Daniel Gorman-

Professor David Deming, a doctor in education and economics at Harvard University, conducted an interesting study where he concluded with some data with which we will certainly agree. We have reached a point in our society were to have a job or to aspire to a position of relevance; more than technical skills are needed. Today's social skills are a fundamental pillar in any scenario — a factor of great value in the world of organizations.

We will, therefore, deepen an aspect that decisively determines our way of relating to the world and, therefore, many aspects of our daily lives.

Definition of social skills

Social skills are a set of behaviors that allow us to interact and interact with others effectively and satisfactorily. An interesting aspect about them is that they can be learned, empowered, and developed every day with practice. Although it is true that it will not always be simple due to the degree of complexity that some of them have, it is also not impossible to achieve it.

An important aspect that we must take into account is that culture and sociodemographic variables are essential to train and evaluate social skills, since depending on where we are habits and ways of relating change.

Therefore, it is not only important to have a good repertoire of social skills, but you have to know when and where to put those skills into practice. The latter is known as social competence.

Thus, owning them avoids anxiety in difficult or novel social situations, facilitating emotional communication, problem-solving, and relationship with others, as long as they adapt to the context.

«The emotionally intelligent person has skills in four areas: identifying emotions, use emotions, understand emotions, and regulate emotions. »

-John Mayer-

If certain social skills are lacking, coping with situations will be passive, avoiding them, and accessing the demands of others. But you can also fall into aggression, imposing criteria and violating the rights of others.

Types of social skills
There is a large number of social skills, but in general, we can distinguish two types that include and organize the rest: necessary social skills and complex social skills. Let's see them in detail.

Basic abilities
- **Listen.** Hearing is not the same as listening, only when we can actively, close and empathically attend to the one in front of us, do we shape that

first step of our social interactions. This dimension, however necessary it may seem, is something we usually fail in many cases.
- **Start a conversation**. Curious as it may be, knowing how to generate a correct opening in a conversation always says a lot about us. It requires ease, requires skills of courtesy and closeness, and requires positivity and those communicative skills where it does not seem threatening or insecure, but quite the opposite.
- **Ask a question**. It knows how to ask, knows how to claim, and also makes use of adequate assertiveness. This social competence is one of the first things children are taught in the classroom and the ones that can help us most in our day to day, in almost any context.
- **Give thanks.** Have you met someone who is not able to say thank you? Knowing how to recognize the other is a fundamental dynamic in any personal or professional relationship. It is civility, and it is respect. Let's never forget this great tribute to social skills.
- **Introduce yourself and introduce others.** We do it in our contexts of friendship and family and also in the work or academic field. Knowing how to introduce ourselves or adding others is an essential basic skill.

Complex skills

Keep in mind that it is necessary to learn the first to develop the second type of social skills and that each situation will demand one or the other, depending on their characteristics and difficulty.

- **Empathy and Emotional Intelligence**. At present, these competencies are essential in any dynamic and circumstance. It is another root that nourishes our relationships in an exceptional way and that without a doubt, we must know how to practice effectively.
- **Assertiveness.** We referred to her just now. In a complex world such as social relations, knowing how to defend ourselves with respect, talking about our needs, communicating and listening, claiming rights, and also caring for others is a valuable skill.
- **Ability to define a problem**, negotiates, and evaluate solutions. This dimension is something we should all practice daily and maximize. In this way, we could reach agreements more easily, negotiate, and set goals where both parties win.
- **Ask for help**. Be aware that we do not know everything, that we need advice, support, or other dimensions is an act of maturity. Knowing how to ask for it effectively is an example of a good mastery of social skills.
- **Convince others.** Knowing how to convince is not manipulating. It knows how to argue, connect, and come to an understanding of where to make the other see that certain behavior or act can be more

beneficial. Creating impact and doing it with respect is an art worth learning.

What are social skills?

Social skills are a very broad term, and in emotional intelligence, they refer to skills needed to effectively deal with and influence other people's emotions.

At first glance, this may seem like operation, but in practice, it is as easy as understanding people to feel better and more positive by smiling.

Social skills can be thought of as the last piece of the emotional intelligence puzzle.

The development of emotional intelligence begins with understanding our own emotions and behaviors through self-awareness.

Raising awareness allows you to manage emotions with self-control and use them to achieve your goals with self-motivation.

To be more easily understood, we can divide social skills into 7 types of skills:

Persuasion Skills

The persuasion is the art of enthusing others to buy our ideas or proposals for action.

Persuasive people are able to understand the emotions of people in a situation and adjust their communication to attract those involved.

Communication skills

Communication is vital for emotional intelligence. You need to be able to listen to others and convey your own thoughts and feelings.

Communicative leaders are open to hearing about the issues and don't want to be told only about the good news. They deal with difficult issues immediately and do not allow problems to rot.

Conflict Management Skills

Conflicts and misunderstandings can arise at any time in a team, often they seem to come out of nowhere.

Good managers are able to bring divergences to light and resolve them. They stimulate debate and open discussion, reducing cliques and hidden problems.

They help each party involved in the conflict to recognize each other's positive intent and logical position. They always seek win-win solutions.

Leadership skills

It may seem odd to include leadership skills as part of social skills. Of course, emotional intelligence is part of leadership, not the other way around.

However, researchers describe leadership skills as the ability of the individual to articulate a vision and to excite others with it.

What's more, they characterize leadership as the ability to influence others to come along with you. That is, for scholars, to lead is not necessary to have a formal leadership position, just be able to support and guide the performance of colleagues, keeping them accountable.

Change Management Skills

We all know that change is naturally stressful for everyone involved.

But leaders with social skills are good catalysts for change. They turn threats and obstacles into exciting opportunities.

They also recognize the need for change and remove their barriers. To do so, they challenge the status quo and act proactively by leading their team by example.

Relationship Skills

It is vital for the leader to know how to build and maintain relationships with others, whether they are subordinates, peers or superiors.

Having relationship skills means being able to build and maintain a strong network of contacts and connections. Leaders with this ability often have many friends among their co-workers.

To build strong relationships, leaders show genuine interest in the people around them. They want to know more about people truly and without falsehood.

Collaboration and cooperation skills

There are some people who work well in teams. These people tend to see interpersonal relationships as important as the task itself, that is, they value people as much as the outcome.

That's why leaders with good cooperative skills share their goals and work closely with the team to build a plan to achieve them. Thus they promote a cooperative climate in which everyone is invited to contribute.

In this way, they attract and engage team members in a common goal while building the team's identity.

The 3 Great Axes of Social Skills

1. Trust, an important element

There is no way to trust others unless we first trust ourselves. This is one of the big questions of social skills that, unfortunately, many people have not yet developed and not cultivated.

This often happens because there is a whole history of learning that leads us to doubt the value we have or, on the contrary, to believe in all our value and potential.

Self-esteem and self-confidence lay their foundation in the early years of life. The relationship with parents is fundamental in this construction. The most common is that if parents have personal difficulties in this field, so will their children. It is not a mathematical equation, it is a trend.

Now it is always possible to change the situation and develop greater confidence in yourself. Experts advise avoiding very fierce self-criticism and negative thoughts about oneself and others.

In addition, learning to express emotions out loud and accurately as possible can also help. On the other hand, learning to maintain a high body posture and not expecting to feel totally safe to act can also be helpful.

2. Communication, a fundamental aspect

Another very important issue of social skills is the ability to communicate. This is almost tautological because it is quite obvious that if we do not develop our communicative skills, we can hardly establish fluid links with others.

The key here is not learning how to make flowery, fiery speeches, learning to convince others, or being experts in oratory. It is to perceive and communicate feelings.

The best way to communicate with others is to talk based on our emotions. It is not rational communication, but emotional communication that allows us to build better relationships with others. So one of the great axes of social skills is being able to convey what we feel and who we are.

Being able to show our feelings and emotions without filters, without fear, without precaution fosters empathy. It is also a deciding factor in generating closeness with others. In fact, it contributes significantly to others also opening their inner world to us, and allowing us to enter it.

3. Connection, the key to healthy bonds

Connecting with others is being present in their lives and knowing how to understand others from their point of view, not from ours. This requires high acceptability.

As with the case of self-confidence and self-esteem, it is impossible to accept others if we cannot accept ourselves before. That is, to recognize and admit our strengths and all our defects with tranquility and ease.

Connecting with each other is possible only if we know how to establish empathy. To achieve this goal, the first step is to know how to listen. This implies not judging, not being conditioned to listen in a certain way by characteristics of our interlocutor.

One must allow the other to be himself while expressing himself. Listening to what you are saying without thinking about something else and not wanting to change what the other is thinking, modify or question what we are hearing and the thought you are expressing.

One tip that can help right now is to ask yourself what the person talking to you wants or needs. It is about understanding what the other is feeling, and what they are trying to express to you. Genuine listening is the basis for an effective connection that will enrich your life as well as the person speaking to you.

Social skills have to do with structuring ourselves better , being closer to ourselves, to our essence. As a result, we will be more open and more receptive to others.

CHAPTER TWO
Why Is Good Social Skills Management So Important?

Social skills are the set of behaviors and attitudes that a person performs in the face of interaction with other individuals; they are formed by the expression of opinions, feelings, and desires. They are part of our nature. Therefore, they develop from the first months of life and are present in all evolutionary stages.

People are social beings, so we inevitably have to relate to others to survive. Therefore, social skills are necessary because everyone likes to have friends, a relationship, that they appreciate ... in case of lack of such skills social relationships can become a source of discomfort and stress by not knowing how to interact with other people.

In fact, studies show that those without them tend to suffer more depressions and episodes of anxiety for not controlling relationships with the environment. Therefore, if we know and optimize our social skills, we will have greater success since we will have greater control in the relations with whom we interact day by day.

Social skills are learned from a very early age, so both parents and educators have a significant role in this field. Like most of the lessons we learn throughout our lives, we acquire them through the following mechanisms:

- **Through experience:** when we put into practice some skill and verify that we get a positive response from other people.
- **Through observation:** we acquire skills when we see behaviors that have worked for other people, and we begin to put them into practice.
- **Through verbal learning:** this learning occurs when another person tells us how to behave in a social context.

For us to adapt satisfactorily to the different situations that are presented to us on a daily basis, it is essential to have a good repertoire of social skills. Then we will be able to generate useful links with other people, as well as other critical aspects that are related to life satisfaction, such as defending our opinions and expressing our feelings.

The two most essential skills, due to their high utility, that must be worked on are empathy and assertiveness. Assertiveness is vital to develop in the social field in a satisfactory way. This consists in expressing personal opinions adequately, defending one's rights even when others have a different point of view. On the contrary, less assertive people are those who do not say what they think or accept everything that other individuals tell them. Also, those who aggressively (if only verbally) try to impose their opinions without respecting those of others.

Examples of people with difficulties in social skills are those who have problems communicating with others, and they have trouble transmitting their emotions, they are uncomfortable when they relate to people they don't know, they don't know how to say "no" when they ask them for favor...

In this respect, it is essential to know that people can be assertive in an area of our life and not in others. For example, we can have excellent social skills with our partner but at work have difficulty saying no to a partner or behaving aggressively with friends ... these skills are given in a given context since they vary depending on the culture, historical moment as well as the concrete situation in which we find ourselves. These differences are what because of the cultural clashes that occur when we find ourselves in a culture different from that of origin.

Much of the problems we have in today's society result in a deficit of social skills, since there are few psychological disorders in which the social area is not involved, to a greater or lesser extent. It is essential to pay attention and evaluate how we develop with others, and if our social relationships are satisfactory. Successful relationships with our friends, bosses, co-workers or partners will, in turn, make us feel valued and respected, which improves our self-esteem and is directly related to how happy we are in our day to day.

Once all this has been explained and considering that there are people with better social skills than others, the question arises whether they can be improved. The good thing is that everything we believe as a skill can be learned and developed with practice. Experts in communication and psychology agree that aspects such as the correct management of emotions, effective communication, and empathy with others can be learned. There are also other concepts that we can work together with, such as active listening, kindness, body posture, intonation, and the language used, the look, the smile, being able to make and receive constructive criticism, courtesy, empathy, emotional intelligence ... Depending on our needs,

As we mentioned above, having a good repertoire of social skills opens many doors to personal success, since it facilitates job, family, couple, and friends' satisfaction ... being directly related to so many critical aspects of our life, it is essential to know if we have a good repertoire of skills; otherwise, it would be advisable to go to a psychology professional to help us improve them based on our specific case.

The importance of Social Skills

Empathy

A column on which social ability is based is "empathy" understood as putting oneself in the place of the other, but not from our point of view, but from the point of view of the other, understanding their expectations, their emotions, their beliefs, your desires, your behaviors...

To achieve this empathy, it is essential to listen and observe the person you want to understand. In active listening, the information that comes from the other person is processed, both verbal and nonverbal information. During the listening, messages should be sent to the speaker to make him see that we understand "feed-back" or in his case, ask for clarification of what we do not understand. It also helps us understand others remember how they acted or felt in situations similar to the one we were at a given time.

Assertiveness

On the other hand, there are our interests, that is, what we want to achieve, what we expect from others. We may ask for help in some matter, that we want a pleasant conversation, a loving relationship, to give an order to a worker ... in any case, our aspirations must be realistic. At this point, it is necessary to know ourselves, our limitations, our abilities, and our emotions.

Once we have an idea as tight as possible of the position of the other person, and we have defined what our aspirations are, we will be able to act; now we can be assertive.

Being assertive means communicating our opinions, ideas desires to others ... clearly but not aggressively. This is the best way to achieve our social goals.

Fights between teenagers, relatives who do not speak, coworkers who become unfair competition, conflicting divorces, arguments out of tune...

There are endless situations that become unbearable, with consequences on stress and health that if at the time, they had been treated in a socially acceptable manner would not have occurred.

The conversation

Within the social skills is the conversation. A conversation should start with the greeting, and the presentation in case the interlocutors are unknown. The greeting must be appropriate to the circumstances and the type of relationship you have with the other person, you can go from hello and a handshake to an affectionate kiss depending on the case.

During the conversation, you should listen actively, that is, show interest in what is said, ask for clarification of what is not understood, respect the turn of the word ... At the same time, we will make our intervention clearly and seeking the listening of others.

The conversations end with a farewell, which, like the greeting, depends on the situation in which we find ourselves. It is important to know the peculiarities of the situation to adjust the greeting and farewell to her. An encounter in a hospital is not the same as on the beach.

It also favors the social relationship to be grateful, kind, smiling, apologize ... all at the right times, and without being excessively complacent. Kindness, for example, could cause rejection both by default and by excess.

Importance of social skills in the company

Companies are no longer satisfied with having in their professional ranks with great knowledge, experts in processes, in markets, or in any other subject. In addition to this, they currently demand social and personal skills that set of strategies learned that help us to act and interact with others in an effective way and oriented to the achievement of our goals. Today we are going to focus on social skills in organizations.

Why are new social skills and concrete attitudes demanded in companies?

In the 21st century, we face a new economic and social paradigm, a globalized environment that demands closeness, with large doses of uncertainty, with an increasingly informed consumer, who wants to interact with the company, with great environmental and social challenges and with contexts as changing as often turbulent. A situation in which to achieve a competitive advantage in the market, we must not only know how to manufacture the product but also know and meet the expectations of the customer (internal or external), of the shareholders, of the company, of the environment, etc. And these are challenges that require a lot of social intelligence in our companies.

What are the social skills most demanded by companies?

Although each case and each context will be unique, we can highlight five useful social skills for corporations.

- **The ability to communicate.** Without fluid communication, it is not possible to maintain positive work climates; it is more difficult to influence customer decisions, negotiate with partners, or simply transmit timely information at the right time. A fluid communication, verbal and nonverbal, grease the structures of organizations and allows efficient operation. Listening actively, empathizing with the interlocutor, being assertive and showing expressiveness and interest in a sincere and balanced way are some basic tips to have this social ability.

- **Leadership,** as the ability to influence people in their behaviors and direct them towards the common goal. Although it is true that many people are born with almost innate leadership skills, this much-needed skill can also be practiced in the workgroups. Working aspects such as the ability to work in a team, delegate, give feedback, know how to motivate, determine objectives, goals, and priorities, be flexible or convey confidence to our employees are key points to improve our leadership.
- **Flexibility** understood not only as of the ability to adapt to different situations - not always positive - but also related to change orientation and negotiation. And, linking with this skill, we would talk about creativity and innovation capacity, like that social ability that enables us to generate new ideas that add value, to do things differently to make them better. Creativity and innovation can be worked with a multitude of techniques and dynamics (mind maps, brainstorming, etc.) but some basic tips to promote this ability have more to do with: clearing our minds of limiting beliefs, learning to question what, the how and why of our activities, read, learn and exchange experiences and, among other things, have fun and relax.
- **Resilience.** This term, taken from physics, tells us about the human capacity to face adversities and not only overcome them but get stronger. A resilient organization is one that faces uncertainty, crises, and critical situations and not only

overcomes them but also becomes positive as a result of these events. Resilience as a social skill that we have in organizations is linked to attitudes of tenacity, effort, optimism, and improvement.

- **The ability to work with enthusiasm and passion**. The magic ingredients The illusion would be the hope of achieving a desired and attractive objective. Something closely linked to motivation and commitment when transposing the concept to the world of business. Passion is an intense feeling that guides the will towards someone or something. Again, an attitude linked to motivation. Passion is the engine of perseverance and of the orientation to achieve results. How to work these items is something complex, but that we can associate with optimism.

Importance of Social Skills in Children

Social skills are a set of behaviors that allow us to function effectively in social situations, being able to establish appropriate relationships with others, and resolve conflicts. These skills begin to develop from the earliest childhood, thanks to the relationships that children develop with the people who care for them and will continue throughout the development based on the experiences they have with their peers. They are loaded with emotions, feelings, ideas, and subjective perceptions that will influence behaviors that unfold in interactions with others.

The importance of social skills lies in the child's adaptation to the different environments in which he/she develops: school, family, peer group ... Facilitating such adaptation or making it difficult, influencing their self-esteem and self-confidence. Therefore, if the first years of life are the foundations on which the child's personality is built and does not have the necessary capabilities for adequate adaptation to their social environments, causing inadequate self-concept and low self-esteem, we find ourselves with great difficulty that will continue beyond childhood, especially striking in adolescence.

The human being is a social being by nature, a deficit in social skills usually becomes something painful for children and adolescents, who see how their relationships with others become very complicated and sometimes causing a rejection of the same or aggressive behaviors and inadequate.

There are many capacities that form social skills; among them, we find:

- Conflict resolution
- Emotional self-control
- Assertiveness
- Communication
- Cooperation
- Empathy ...

All these capacities are important throughout our lives. However, two of them acquire especially important nuances as the child grows and goes through puberty and adolescence: empathy and assertiveness.

Empathy can be understood as the ability to place yourself in another person's point of view and act according to the feelings of the other. It requires adequate emotional understanding from childhood and is the key to success in social performance. Assertiveness is the ability to defend one's rights and interests without harming others. Empathy and assertiveness go hand in hand, and finding the balance between both skills is essential to successfully resolve the social conflicts that will arise in our lives.

Importance of Social Skills in Relationships

When a couple begins to report their relationship grievances, in many cases, a greater tendency to note "partner" misperceptions is apparent than a description of individual difficulties and interaction. Even so, it is frequent the divergence of the answers of each one in the description of daily events.

In order to improve this relationship, a first point to note refers to the understanding of the functional analysis of events, in which situations would be analyzed based on their antecedents, responses, and consequences, and, therefore, both individuals that make up the couple become involved.

With this understanding in place, we need a more specific analysis of events in which appropriate reinforcement increases in frequency, as well as a reduction in aversive behaviors (which lead to withdrawal) between the couple. For this, it is important to identify individual behaviors of both categories, in order to bring benefits to the relationship. Faced with eventual mismatches and difficulties, we are faced with the need for clear, open, and adjusted dialogue between the couple. That is, we are talking about the need for social skills, including conversation, for each spouse.

When it comes to communication, what is said by each spouse, how it is expressed, and at what time, are essential and structural components that need to be measured and adjusted according to each stakeholder. That is, rather than a single, pre-established formula for marital success, a construction that respects both and is unique to that couple becomes essential.

Knowing how to communicate assertively, skillfully expressing one's own desires and feelings, has a specificity with regard to couples, since such interaction involves a continuous and intense living, bringing an atmosphere of intimacy and permissiveness that can help or hinder assertive communication. , which takes into consideration not only myself but the other.

Also, when it comes to love relationships, we need to remember that we are talking about two people coming from different life histories and, therefore, with different learning and behavioral repertoires that will intertwine their lives for the purpose of a two-way life project.

For such a meeting to be more harmonious, it will be essential for partners to have self-knowledge and develop new learning not only about assertive communication but also broader social skills.

According to Caballo (1999), some classes of responses considered effective are: "start and maintain conversations; ability to express love, pleasure and affection; no one's own rights and duties; ask for favors; refuse requests; accept compliments; ability to express personal opinions, including discordant ones; ability to accept dissenting opinions; ability to express discomfort, dislike or boredom; apologize or admit ignorance; request change in the behavior of the other; face criticism; among others.

Exercising in daily practice, such as skills, is challenging and involves continuous learning, training, and exercise. But it will be just such an investment that can provide clear, empathic communication that emphasizes mutual validation and that builds a bond of closeness and unity between spouses consistently and robustly, meaning an investment in that relationship on a daily and ongoing basis.

CHAPTER THREE
How to Improve Social Skills

Many of us feel misplaced or disappointed in certain social situations.

As indicated above it is necessary to develop social skills to achieve optimal social relations, and that is why it is important:

- gain confidence,
- develop greater assertiveness,
- work our self-esteem to express ourselves firmly and effectively,
- handle emotional self-control techniques,
- work our emotional intelligence,
- and know how to relax during more tense dialogues,

It will help us to achieve satisfactory relationships with others.

The importance of assertiveness

Assertive Answers Many people complain about their social and personal life, feeling too passive, aggressive, or hostile in handling their interpersonal problems.

The lack of assertiveness, we can face situations passive, so avoiding them and accessing the needs of others or, conversely, falling into aggression infringing the rights of others.

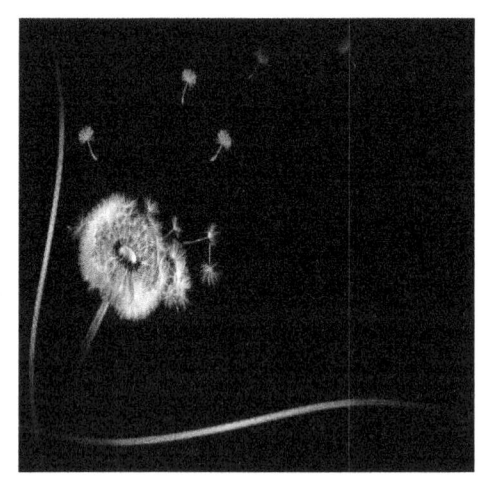

To acquire social skills, first of all, it is necessary to develop "assertive arguments" of application in various interpersonal conflicts and rehearse those arguments and deliver them with an expressive voice and body language.

- Lack of assertiveness is the decisive cause of feelings of restlessness and dislocation.
- Assertiveness is the product of a set of attitudes learned and communication skills that can change and improve.

A large part of our desirable or undesirable behavior depends on the experiences of education or learning. And our learning continues because we are constantly adapting to the changing environment. The human being can modify and learn new ways that will serve to replace the previous and less productive ones.

Are You An Assertive Person?

The assertive term has several connotations:

- Ability to express feelings
- Choose how to act
- Choose how to defend rights at the right time
- Disagree when you think it is important to do so
- Enhance self-esteem
- Help develop self-confidence
- Carry out plans to modify one's behavior
- Ask others to change their offensive behavior.

To improve your social skills and be an assertive person, you can start from the following rules:

- Use expressive speech. Express your personal tastes and interests spontaneously and accurately. E.g., I like this food. I love your outfit. I think.... When it is considered convenient.
- Talk about yourself. You can simply mention your achievements when you consider it worth doing.
- Say hello, cordially.
- Accept compliments instead of disagreeing with them.
- Use facial language appropriately
- Disagree peacefully.
- Request clarification and ask why
- Actively express your disagreement
- Defend your rights
- Be persistent
- Avoid justifying each opinion

By being assertive, you can learn to negotiate with respect to mutually satisfactory solutions in a wide variety of interpersonal problems. Our human rights arise from the idea that we were all created equally in a moral sense and should treat each other as equals.

There are 4 phases in the development and learning of more assertive behaviors:

- **Project:** Remember and project yourself in previous conflict situations in which I fail to affirm you, to see what the most common situational aspects are. (identification of who, when and what)
- **Analyze:** Analyze the degree of threat and confusion you feel in these postponing situations and choose a specific "half threat" scene, as an immediate approach to your self-improvement program (assess the discomfort in intimidating situations in detail and think about how to focus efforts to become more assertive)
- **Reflect:** Critically observe your behavior to see what emotions, negative statements and self-images maintain your lack of assertiveness in the "problem-scene" and what you could do to change them (Examination of emotional reactions and feelings. Think rationally about the consequences of assertiveness)
- **Express yourself:** Finally, plan an argument or message to remedy your problematic situation and learn to express yourself in an affirmative way.

Some specific strategies to interact with others more assertively, which can help improve your social skills:

- Be more objective in observing others and oneself in certain situations.

- Plan a campaign to establish contracts for favorable behavioral changes in yourself and others.
- Express yourself with assertive language, qualified voice, and body movements appropriate to the circumstance.
- Continuity in the consequences of the contract that you have negotiated with another person.
- Handle yourself in occasional situations of crucial type when you interact with an offensive person.

The Importance of Our Self-Esteem

Second, we can improve our self-esteem — many people who feel misplaced manifest a negative concept of themselves. Throughout their lives, they have self-taught as shy, inept, or passive ... "I am too weak," ... "I am stupid" ... "I could never speak in front of all these people" ... through a systematic approach to positive thinking about one, you will begin to improve self-image and be more assertive. That will help us improve our social skills.

Do You Have Good Self-Esteem?

People typically put three major obstacles between themselves and the assertiveness goal:

- The negative image of herself
- Fear imposed on conflict situations

- Communication inability

Our Self-Esteem Or Our Self-Concept Is A Product Of Experience.

We all acquire our self-concept in almost the same way. As we grow up, our parents, teachers, and other adults impart us through rules, habits, values , and forms of behavior corresponding to their culture. These rules tell us what behaviors are considered appropriate, and we are developing the image we have of ourselves.

Whether or not being assertive is determined by our self-concept, by the mental picture (conscious or unconscious) that we maintain our strengths, our weaknesses, and our personality. Our self-concept is usually revealed in the way we compare ourselves with the people of relevance around us.

We make such self-judgments not only with respect to our skills in sports, arts, and culture but also in regard to our social and personal adaptation to the environment to which we belong. We can say that your self-concept is wrapped in a set of descriptions and images of scenes of positive achievements or scenes of failures.

Your self-assessments are essential because they influence most areas of your behavior and defend the limits of what you are trying. You probably avoid the activities in which your self-concept and self-esteem predict that you can perform as negatively as to feel humiliated. The effect of a negative self-concept generally leads to limiting what we want to prove, frustrating opportunities for growth and enjoyment.

Many people are crushed by images of failures experienced in their social clashes. The images that prevent people from acquiring assertiveness are based on memories of previous weaknesses and failures, as well as bindings in specific situations.

In sum, manifestations and negative images continually inhibit non-assertive people. By concentrating on negative evaluations of their person, these people lose valuable growth opportunities and enjoy the situations that surround their lives.

How to learn social skills?
Improving these skills is a process of acquiring habits, and as such, it requires training and repetition of the behavior. In adults and children, it has been shown that it is possible to develop and acquire social skills.

Below we have listed a list of concrete strategies that have proven effective in improving your social and emotional relationships. You can perform tests in your environment, such as small exercises that help acquire social skills. They will help you feel more confident and start interacting with new people without fear.

Strategies to improve our social skills:
- **Learn to activate the look:** It is very instructive to observe what you think of a person and how he reacts to you. Many people believe they look directly at others, but it is not so.
- **Initiate greetings correctly with mindfulness:** Although most of us would like to be cordially managed, we tend to avoid the social relationship because we fear being rejected.
- **Give and accept authentic compliments:** Rewarding other people is a way of telling them that you value their friendship, that you enjoy their company, and that you want them to feel happy. One of the most common ways is to give compliments. Unfortunately, many people often skip to encouraging someone who provides a genuine compliment. Learn to accept authentic compliments and reward your interlocutor. It is also the case that you need to learn to make compliments to others properly.
- **Request clarification**: Sometimes, we are not able to interpret the comments that someone makes in our regard, and we are not at all sure of

what he told us, but we do notice that such comments make us feel restless. It is important to learn to ask others for clarification of enigmatic or incomprehensible manifestations. Sometimes there are people who release aggressive hints, but they get stunned when asked to clarify what they have said and said exactly what they want. Although reeducating with a reliable critic can be important for our development, these critics often sin from poorly informed or unable to hold opinions. Assertive people can accept and make use of criticism to change when it is appropriate to do so.

- **Ask for help:** Do you feel saturated with work, and would you like others to help you? Can you ask for help without feeling guilty or fearful? An important assertive behavior refers to the fact of requesting help when one feels overworked.
- **Demonstrate your legitimate rights:** For example, Maria felt guilty because she thought her intolerance for small things was unreasonable. By writing them and sharing them with other people, he understood that she was not as mean as she supposed, but that she had the right to express herself with respect to things, big or small.
- **Participate in conversations:** If you have difficulty engaging in a conversation, there are a lot of exercises that help take the conversation to topics in your domain. It is an art to tell an experience or develop an opinion. If you want to give an opinion, it is convenient that the opinion is

duly documented. The conversations are carried out on 3 different levels, and it is important to know what level to use in each situation (explained below).

- **Use body language that says "yes or no" as needed**: To reach assertiveness, you must be aware of the messages that your body can deliver. Through facial expressions and body movements, we usually transmit fear, worry, sadness, surprise, suspicion, happiness ... This body language has a strong impact on others. In order to study your body language, observe what your body does and what effect your posture, your movements, your gestures, and your facial expressions have on the people you speak with.
- **Abandon self-righteousness:** Passive people, not very assertive, think they are obliged to justify every opinion or manifestation they make with rational arguments. When someone questions or criticizes them, they feel compelled to defend themselves with prolonged reasons. Although giving reasons is a valuable educational practice, it has limited value in interpersonal relationships, in which feelings and rights are as important as reasons. We have every right to say: "I think that way."
- **Use expressive language to demonstrate our feelings:** Shy people rarely speak expressively about their feelings, because of which they appear discolored and lack of interest, consequently, they have great difficulty making friends. Friendship

tends to develop through mutual self-revelation, accepting and giving back relevant author information provided by the other person, and giving similar information to the interlocutor. This self-information consists especially of manifestations concerning our life and our goals, as well as opinions, ideas, and feelings. People who do not know how to express their feelings are often identified as "introverted" or "cold." You can practice the open expression of feelings

How to teach social skills to children and adolescents

Although this process usually occurs unconsciously in young children, it is also possible to do it voluntarily through a social skills training program. We know that many children and adolescents have little knowledge of social skills to interact correctly with others. But as previously commented, social skills can be developed. We have listed some strategies that help in learning correct social skills:

- Select a single social skill. For example, undertake to greet correctly.
- Talk about the need for social skills, so they understand why they are important.
- Teach the skill, such as learning to relax.

- Pause and reflect
- Implement the skill; for example, carry out a conversation with an assertiveness approach.
- Review and think, talk about specific situations.

Helpful and Practical Advice for Improving Social Skills

How to react to criticism? Do you have a wide repertoire of communicative skills? Did you know that it is possible to improve social skills? Our social skills are learned behaviors. Improving our social skills is as much a necessary task as learning to walk, read, and write.

As we have seen before, social skills are all those necessary behaviors that allow us to interact and relate to others effectively and satisfactorily. Here are some communicative techniques that will allow you to improve your social skills so that you can improve relationships with those around you, so you can learn how to resolve personal conflicts.

Useful and practical advice for improving social skills

1. **Scratched disc technique.** It consists of consistently repeating the main idea of what we want to express, or the phrases of our requests, i.e., repeating the same phrase more than once, regardless of what the other person says.

- "We're offering a new promotion from..." - "Fine, but I'm not interested. Thank you. "-" How are you sure? "- "I get it, but I don't want to buy it, thank you very much. "-" I can make a special price... "-"No, thanks. I do not care,".

2. Negative Affirmation. It is a way of reacting to fair criticism without giving many justifications. - "You did the exercise very slowly." - "True, I could have done faster, I'm sorry."

3. Negative question. It is useful for recognizing others' thoughts, facilitating communication when we are criticized. Help arouse sincere criticism from others. - "What bothers you about my way of speaking?" - "What's wrong with going to the theater?" - "What's the matter with the way I dress?"

4. Ask questions. The questions are meant to help each other perceive an impulsive reaction. - "Are you upset about something?"

5. Disarm the anger. Ignore the content of the angry message (insults, criticism, etc.) and focus your attention and conversation on the fact that the person is upset. For example, we may shift the focus of the content conversation to some process we may observe in the person, such as an emotion or behavior that they are displaying.

6. Sandwich Technique. One of the most effective techniques for improving social skills is to start with a positive aspect, then an aspect that could be improved and finally to end with words of encouragement and confidence. "I know that you are striving to change your attitude towards... and you realize that you have improved. I believe you can, yes, improve on... (Aspect to be improved). I'm sure you will make it soon. "

7. Repeat what the other person feels. We repeat what the other person says to give them the message we understand, but without showing any agreement with what they say. - "I know it's very important to you that I lend you the car, but..."

8. Show affection. Giving affection is critical to maintaining a healthy relationship. Sometimes you need to do something other than just express yourself with words, such as a hug, a kiss, a caress, or even a smile. Feelings can also improve social skills.

9. Praise. Just as we like to receive compliments, so do others. So we need to know how to compliment it.

10. Messages from the "I." "I" messages are used to give our opinion or express our beliefs to each other rather than generalize. If for me, something is one way, it need not be the same for the other. "I think...", "I believe...", "In my opinion..."

11. Keep conversations. It is to maintain the balance between listening and speaking, making our participation enjoyable. Some helpful behaviors are: looking into the eyes, respecting the turn, giving signals that you are listening (nodding, for example, talking about something related to the person speaking, warning about changes in the subject, etc.)

In general, we can always improve social skills with some aspects of how we treat others. Above all, one must be prepared and put into practice all of the above.

How to Develop Your Social Skills with Body Language

Reinforcing:

Social skills are classes of varied behaviors that you can issue with the intention of dealing with interpersonal situations appropriately. These classes include Social Communication Skills, which I started by addressing the skills of starting and ending a conversation.

Still, with the proposal to combine Body Language with Social Skills, I will give tips on nonverbal behavior in two other great communication skills:

- Abilities to gratify and praise;
- Abilities to ask and give feedback in interpersonal relationships.

Reward and praise skills

Social competence to gratify is often associated with charismatic people, popular people, and good leaders. When you compliment someone, you are responding positively to their action or trait. A compliment can be seen as recognition and positive reinforcement; as a motivating agent. However, care should be taken that compliment is not viewed as flattery or manipulation, as the effect of complement may be the opposite of what you expect to achieve.

For your praise to be well accepted by people, there needs to be perfect synchronization between the triad of reason, feeling, and action. That is, what you feel and think should be consistent with your body and speech.

Signs of incongruity should be avoided so that your compliments do not sound like falsehood.

Signs of incongruity

Signs that indicate incongruity are identified when someone's speech is not in sync with their body; the synchrony between body and speech gives the idea of harmony, truth, and clarity of ideas.

While praising someone, do not shake your head or shake your shoulders unevenly, as it may indicate uncertainty and lack of firmness in what you have just said.

The smile

A real smile, when it's time to make a compliment, is a key piece, but a smile in which only the lips are pulled sideways, the famous " yellow smile ", can send a message contrary to the intended one.

Crossed arms

Arms crossed can have many meanings - sometimes, the environment you find yourself in can be very cold, but by the time you compliment someone if you are arms crossed, you may be getting the idea that you are not completely honest or not. be giving that compliment spontaneously.

Receiving compliments

Receiving a compliment may seem like an easier skill; after all, we usually think that just saying thank you. Expressing gratitude is exactly what we should do after receiving a compliment, but many people fail right now: some factors, such as shyness or self-esteem issues, end up disrupting these social skills.

Learning to receive a compliment is to value yourself and show that you are aware of your ability. If your body posture does not show your worthiness, it may lead to people not noticing your merit and therefore doubting your ability.

Having an upright posture, keeping your shoulders up and your chin horizontal are all body postures that will help you say, 'I am grateful to have been noticed and recognize my ability.'

Understand nonverbal communications

A skilled social leader is not only dependent on verbal communication. He can understand all types of communication: verbal, nonverbal, written, visual, etc.

To effectively interpret nonverbal cues in your interactions with people, you must be able to recognize how your personal perception filters information.

For this, you need to turn off the voice of your head that is judging people. That way you will be able to read other people and understand what is really happening to them.

Another option for increasing your nonverbal communication skills is to learn about body language and to be aware of people's tone of voice and look.

Have a positive communication

The subordinates closely observe everything their leaders do. No matter if you just get bad news, always act positively.

Avoid making complaints of any kind to the people on your team. If you have a low performing employee, don't expose it to other people, just treat the problem.

What's more, always try to think about solving problems rather than judging or looking guilty. Adopt a positive attitude toward the team and solve problems rather than justifying them.

Make a good impression

Socially intelligent people consider the impression they make on other people in all their interactions.

Considered as one of the most complex elements of social intelligence, managing a reputation requires a careful balance between desired image and authenticity.

Thus, you should try to create a positive image of your reputation in other people in an authentic way.

Therefore, the only solution is to always seek to improve oneself. For this, you must know your values and increase your level of awareness about your behaviors through self-knowledge.

Tips for Developing Your Child's Social Skills

Social skills are a series of skills that help children cope with feelings and establish healthy interpersonal relationships. Through conversations and guidance, you can teach your children to interact with people and respect differences. For this, there are some points that you need to work on day to day.

Identify and control your own emotions

Journalist Daniel Goleman popularized the term "emotional intelligence" in the 1990s. The concept refers to a type of intelligence that involves five pillars: knowing one's emotions, controlling them, motivating oneself, recognizing feelings in others, and Creating Relationships.

Develop verbal language

To be successful in social life, it is important to improve the ability to communicate. In this sense, psychologist and researcher Lawrence E. Shapiro argues that "children need to know how to present themselves, how to develop a personal dialogue, and how to maintain a group conversation." Therefore, the improvement of social skills also involves language learning. Teach them the basic little introductory phrases and help them learn to have conversations with other children.

Develop nonverbal language

For Lawrence E. Shapiro, nonverbal language is a two-way street: "For their social success, children must learn to listen to the nonverbal messages they emit and to decipher the emotions behind others' messages," he says.

Teach children to be part of a group

Children can develop their emotional side as individuals and yet not get along in groups. Therefore, it is important that parents always seek to monitor the social life of their children. According to Lawrence Shapiro, "the inability to join groups during elementary years can be a painful experience for children." Talk to the teachers and make sure your child is having problems in the classroom, looking to intervene if necessary.

Encourage social interaction

This is one of the most important tips. Have your child participate in interaction groups where they can work as a team and explore cooperation and communication. After all, the best way to cultivate these skills is by trying to work them out in practice.
Follow his experiences in these groups and gradually teach, with dialogues, good practices for improving social relationships when he is part of a group of people.

Encourage the good use of technology and games.

Technology can be a great ally for the development of social skills in children. Learning activities such as programming help develop a sense of cooperation and communication in early childhood, as it constantly requires students to seek help from others for problem-solving.

The internet itself can be a good communication tool when used well. Here your child can interact with others, get to know them better, and understand them to gain empathy.

Games also play a key role in this and can bring benefits to the future. Video games, for example, can stimulate skills that the market demands, such as communication and cooperation, with teamwork.

Finally, there are a number of crucial life skills that need to be cultivated so that children can better prepare themselves as adults

Teach yourself to put yourself in others' shoes.

To develop respect and empathy, teach your child to put himself in the shoes of others and to try to understand others' difficulties. This can even be represented in practice with imitation play, for example, so that he understands the extent of this need. The tip is also useful for developing the ability to split.

Instigate self-criticism

Have the children verbally acknowledge their mistakes and admit what they have done. The goal is to develop a sense of self-criticism, self-knowledge, and recognition of one's own failings. Then talk cordially with them and teach why certain actions are wrong and harmful to life in society.

CHAPTER FOUR
How to Behave Like a Social Person

Being a person with the ability to communicate with others, knowing how to speak in meetings, and meeting new people is what defines sociable people.

If, in addition to these qualities, we add certain self-confidence, spontaneity, and desire to live, we can be before a sociable and fun person: that type of people who make us have good times and who manage to arouse the sympathy of almost everyone.

Being sociable: an advantage for different areas of life

In addition to the clear advantages that being sociable can bring in leisure environments, it should also be noted that, increasingly, companies value sociability and communication skills.

In a world where machines replace human work, the virtue of knowing how to communicate well and connect with the interlocutors are becoming important, and it is for this reason that corporations seek professional profiles that empathic and open-minded people that help them to know the tastes of your potential customers or who know how to connect with other companies responsible.

Tricks to be more sociable, fun and empathetic

If you are a little shy or reserved person, you should know that social and communication skills can be learned. In fact, connecting with other people is one of the most trainable capabilities we have. We are social beings by nature, and if you put these tips and tricks into practice, you can improve in this aspect. Tricks to be more sociable, fun and empathetic

If you are a little shy or reserved person, you should know that social and communication skills can be learned. In fact, connecting with other people is one of the most trainable capabilities we have. We are social beings by nature, and if you put these tips and tricks into practice, you can improve in this aspect.

1. The importance of trusting yourself

This may be easy to say, but it is not so easy to put into practice if parts of a little depressed self-esteem or have become accustomed to thinking that meeting people is not your thing. You have to know that we all have things that make us unique and special, curious stories, and a vision of the reality that distinguishes us.

If you are able to value yourself, you can approach those people you want to know for sure, and it will be much easier to connect personally and emotionally.

2. Don't be afraid to talk with strangers

One of the things that will help you decisively to improve your social skills is to throw yourself into the ring and start talking with people you don't know much about. For example, you can try to talk with people who generate more confidence, about topics that are comfortable for you, such as some current news or something that genuinely calls your attention to your interlocutor. You will see how the vast majority of people react positively to your questions.

Gradually, if you practice this point, you will notice that each time it costs you less to start conversations, and you dare to talk with individuals who previously imposed you more.

3. Look in the eyes of your interlocutor

It is important that you get used to having eye contact with the person with whom you speak. Not only will you convey greater confidence in yourself, but it will allow you to connect and generate empathy with your interlocutor.

Also, note that it is very positive that you can have a touch of humor. Surely the person with whom you talk will value your mood and empathize more with you. Of course, it is not a good idea to exceed certain limits in humor. At least in the first contacts, let's use a nice kind of jokes that can't cause discomfort.

4. Be genuinely interested in your interlocutor

Do you like someone else genuinely interested in you? You are very likely to answer yes to this question. We like to feel valued, and therefore we feel good that there are other human beings who want to know us better.

If you like other individuals to be interested in you, the same happens to other people. Therefore, it is a good idea to be the one who encourages interaction. Without the need for it to appear that you are interrogating them, fluid and enjoyable communication can provide you with tools to be more sociable and fun. Above all, it touches themes that can unite, as common interests.

5. Don't just interact with your nearby circle

You should be encouraged to start conversations not only with the people around you most of the time but also with people with whom you agree in more informal contexts and situations. If you always surround yourself and talk to the same circle of people, you will tend to stay in your comfort zone.

Find places and situations where you can meet new people and put into practice your sociability and your ability to communicate and empathize.

6. Keep in touch

If you know someone with whom you would like to meet again on another occasion, do not hesitate to ask for some form of contact (Facebook, phone, email ...). In this way, you will have a quick way to hear from that person again and, if you both want, you can go back somewhere and return to friendship.

In our age of technologies and social networks, many friendships can stay alive over time thanks to this medium. Take advantage of it.

7. Join group activities

If you do activities with more people (such as training courses, team sports, gatherings on a topic that interests you ...), you will be forced to meet new people and cooperate.

This can be very useful if in your daily life you don't have places to expand your horizons. Surely joining one of these groups, or even going to the gym, can be very helpful when developing your sociability.

8. Be someone with whom it's nice to be

Don't underestimate the importance of smiling, being gentle, and having good manners with other people. It is easy to deduce that we are all attracted to those who make us feel good.

This is one of the most important tips if you want to develop your sociability and your empathy because if you are kind, you will notice that others begin to give you the same good treatment back.

9. Practice whenever you can

Your family circle and your closest friends can be a good test bench to open and socialize. All the techniques and tricks mentioned above can be put into practice with them: be interested in their lives, keep in touch if you don't have them close, and empathize with them, do unusual activities...

If you have an exciting and active life, you will not only be more sociable and interesting, but you will attract more people to want to meet you.

10. Don't worry if some interaction doesn't work out as you expected

Losing means to relate to others also means accepting that not everything always goes as Queremos s. In fact, you have to keep in mind that sometimes, the people with whom you will try to interact will not be in the mood. It happens to all of us at some time, and there is no need to turn it over.

Start and end a conversation

Identifying the best time to start a conversation is a very important social skill because often because you don't know how or when to start a conversation, you may miss out on a great social, personal, or professional opportunity. On the other hand, if you don't know how to end a conversation properly, you may receive dislike from your listener.

If you want to raise an issue with someone, it is important first of all to pay attention to the nonverbal signals emitted: if, upon meeting you, the person smiles naturally and gradually - not mechanically - and maintains an open posture - as per example open arms or body approach - there is a great possibility that person will be available for a conversation with you.

Every first contact should begin with a greeting that may vary according to cultural and personal issues - the degree of intimacy between you and someone else, personal characteristics of the caller, etc.

You can start with a greeting, such as a palm greeting facing the speaker, followed by a presentation or explanation of the purpose of a particular conversation. If you know the person and have intimacy for that, a slight touching the arm can create a greater connection between you.

The problem is often not the beginning but the end. I've often seen cases where people didn't know how to end a conversation without seeming inelegant, and this can be very embarrassing. This is where you need to be aware of body signals; they will indicate when a conversation should end. If you've been talking to someone for a while and realize that other person's feet are not toward you, your eyes get lost from time to time and objects such as keys, cell phone, watch get your attention more than they usually do.

Most likely, this is the right time to end the conversation. Appropriately ending date is ideal so that you won't be reminded of how boring clueless that talks too much and doesn't touch.

Knowing how to read a person's nonverbal content causes the conversation to flow naturally until it naturally ends.

CHAPTER FIVE
Verbal and Non Verbal Skills

Communication is of primary importance in the development of humanity. In fact, it is this ability to communicate in such diverse and complex ways that distinguish us from other animals and is considered one of the key features of advanced intelligence. This ability is divided into verbal and nonverbal communication. Although the difference between them is relatively simple to define, it is necessary to understand the importance that each one has when transmitting information.

What is communication?

Communication is given by the exchange of information between at least two individuals, consisting of verbal and/or nonverbal language. That is, when it comes to communicating, you can use one of them separately or apply them together. We can say that communication is effective only if the receiver understands the message the sender wanted to convey. This requires that the message be clear and objective. Keep in mind that the message is the true treasure of communication, and this message can be conveyed verbally or nonverbally. So let's see what the differences between them are.

Verbal communication

The verbal communication can be defined as any spoken or written language, i.e., all messages conveyed through words. It's part of our daily lives, and it has a huge variety as there are around 7,000 languages in the world! In a way, language is different for each of these languages, with different ways of seeing the world. Another highlight is the advent of writing, considered the greatest invention of all time, which allowed information to be documented, thus keeping records for posterity. Thus, it is possible to realize the importance that this type of communication has. And it's not just what you say, but how you say it. Your tone of voice and the volume with which you speak considerably influence communication, making a message more "pleasant or not." While the tone of voice is an element of nonverbal language, spoken words belong to verbal and are very important in communication. Don't fall for this to think they don't matter. After all, it has no body language and tone of voice that fixes the wrong word at the wrong time.

Non-verbal communication

Nonverbal communication is understood by all that does not use words. We have already talked about the tone of voice, but this is just one of the elements of this kind of language.

Another example is body language, which encompasses both body movements and facial expressions. This type of communication has a great influence on speech, being one of the main points of observation for those who want to speak well in public. Hand care, posture, and tone of voice make the difference, giving you more confidence and security.

Nonverbal language has interesting and universal features, such as some gestures (there are several exceptions) that are understood anywhere in the world or even a facial expression of sadness, which is basically the same for everyone. Another excellent example of the application of nonverbal language is in traffic signs.

Have you ever stopped to think that most traffic signs do not have words written on them? Even so, we understand perfectly the message transmitted by them, because we learn as much in the Auto School as by repetition and the conviviality in the society.

It is interesting to realize that we have gotten used to these conventions and find it very strange when any change occurs. Think about it, can you imagine stopping when the traffic light indicates green light? That would be pretty weird, wouldn't it?

A point to note is that this choice was based on our visual perception, which associates red with danger and green with tranquility. Yellow, which is the intermediary between them, thus becomes the sign of attention. But how important is it?

Well, it's based on the way our interpretation of nonverbal messages is made that we develop body language studies, because our mind associates certain gestures with feelings, making communication more or less effective.

Ways to Improve Your Communication Skills

Beware of body language

Say that the discussion is open with arms crossed; say you're listening, but don't take your eyes off the phone. Our nonverbal and unwritten signals often reveal more than we think they do. Whether it is the way you make eye contact or pose during a job interview, you are sure that you are in constant communication, even when you are not saying a word.

One way to be aware of this body language is to think about your toes or adopt a dominant pose that increases your confidence. It's also nice to learn to read other people's body language so you can respond appropriately.

Get rid of conversational "fillers."

"Hum," "ah," "type," and their derivatives do little to improve your speech or everyday conversations. Eliminate them to be more persuasive and/or appear more confident. For this, you can simply try to relax and take a break before speaking. These silences seem more embarrassing to you than to others.

Have a script for casual conversations

Chatting away is an art that many people do not master. Embarrassing silences with people you barely know can be avoided by the FORD method (family, occupation, recreation, and desires). From these topics, you can enjoy chatting topics, such as whose hobbies, whether they have siblings, or what their dream life is. You can also turn a shallow conversation into a denser conversation by sharing information that can help you find something in common with the other person.

Tell a story

Stories are powerful. They activate the brain, make presentations more interesting, make us more persuasive, and may even help us with interviews. Study the secrets of telling a good story, and use conjunctions to structure your narrative.

Ask questions and repeat the other person's words.

Asking questions and repeating the other person's last words shows that you are interested in the conversation and helps clarify points that could be misunderstood. It also assists in small talk to fill awkward silences. Instead of trying to chatter about the weather, ask questions like, "What are your plans for your vacation?" Or "What are you reading lately?" And continue the conversation based on the answers. For good communication, it is more important to be interested than to be interesting.

Get rid of distractions

It is very rude to use the phone while someone is talking to you, or when you are in a meeting with other people. It may be impossible to get rid of all distractions or put technology aside completely, but the effort to engage fully in conversation greatly improves our communication with others.

Adjust your message to your audience

The best communicators adjust the way they speak based on who is listening. You would probably use a different style of communication with your co-workers x your boss or with your husband/wife x your children. Always try to keep the other person's perspective in mind when you are getting your message across.

Be brief and specific

Keep in mind what you want to say and use a few words. For example, when sending an email, think about the purpose or reason for sending it the information you want to convey and the response you want to get. Simple. A good policy for both written and verbal communication is to use the 7 Cs of communication: be clear, concise, concrete, correct, consistent, complete, and courteous.

Have empathy

Communication is a two-way street. Practicing seeing things from the other's point of view can reduce the difficulty and anxiety that sometimes arises when trying to truly communicate with someone. Developing empathy helps you better understand even what hasn't been said in words, and respond more effectively.

Listen

Finally, according to most of the points above, the best thing you can do to improve your communication skills is to learn to listen - really pay attention and let the other person talk without interrupting you. It's hard, but it improves the conversation even if the communication styles are not the same, and causes the other person to listen to you carefully as well.

Dealing With Awkward Silence in Conversation

The human being is an incredible animal for the simple fact of having the power to talk; Thanks to speech we can both cooperate and persuade or even defend our perception of the world, or simply meet people and seduce. However, and despite the fact that the range of possibilities offered by the art of the word is almost unlimited, there are situations in which none of that matters, because we block ourselves when trying to chat with someone.

The awkward silences are situations that many want to avoid, but that, incomprehensibly, appear again and again in the daily lives of many people. However, by training in certain social skills, it is possible to master some simple tricks to avoid those awkward silences.

Social skills to avoid awkward silences

You are talking to a person with whom you had just crossed a few words before, and everything is going perfect: during the first minute, you realize that you have been able to easily overcome that phase of uncertainty in which you must decide how to start the conversation, and for the moment everything seems to go on wheels. However, there comes the point where the subject you are talking about apparently no longer gives of itself, and that odious awkward silence appears. What has failed?

As we will see, there are different answers to the previous question. To explain it, we will see several strategies that help prevent these small relational problems. Of course, in all of them, it is assumed that the conversation has already begun. If you are also interested in knowing how to start talking to someone with whom there is not much trust, it is better to go to this other

Without more, let's see what are the steps to follow to have fluent conversations and in which the naturalness prime.

1. Emphasize positive aspects of the other

It may seem strange, but flattery has a relationship with awkward silences or, rather, with the absence of awkward silences. And it is that many times these "dead spots" of the conversation are due neither more nor less because either we or our interlocutors have adopted a defensive attitude, something that on the other hand, is frequent when the person with The one that is spoken. In the face of uncertainty, we unconsciously think that it is best not to expose vulnerabilities through what we say.

Thus, flattery is a simple and easy way to make a good part of those defenses fall apart. The consequence of this is that the person who receives these positive assessments pronounced out loud will open more, be explained more extensively, and at the same time, make us feel more comfortable.

2. Start conversations about something that interests the other

It is an easy way to avoid awkward silences. On the one hand, it allows to skip those phases of the formal conversation composed of topics that do not have to be of interest (time, work in general, etc.), and on the other, it makes our interlocutors feel comfortable talking about something that excites them and about what they have many ideas. For example, you can talk about hobbies, news in an area of interesting news, etc. Thus, the answers are unlikely to be short.

3. Don't talk fearing the breaks

One of the key aspects of the awkward silences is that, in order for them to exist, almost any pause in the conversation must be interpreted as a "failure," a symptom that the people involved in the dialogue are not connecting. However, this does not have to happen; A pause can mean many other things.

For example, it is possible that to give emphasis to a statement, it is accompanied by a pause set there deliberately so that the forcefulness of the response is enhanced and, therefore, that we have a very clear opinion on what is talking.

Many times, awkward silence appears when this occurs, and we are not able to draw attention to the expressive power of this fact: we simply say a phrase and shut up because we fail to conceive of another possible answer. However, on certain issues where one might expect different opinions from ours, the simple fact of having created that silence is itself another topic of conversation, since it gives rise to explaining why we are so sure of what we say.

4. Get used to comment without fear

Anyone will be willing to end a conversation if all we contribute to the dialogue is one question after another. Interrogations are not to anyone's liking and are the most conducive context to make them seem uncomfortable silences. The solution to this is simple: avoid asking questions all the time.

In practice, if what you say is interesting or expresses an original point of view, the effect of these contributions to the dialogue will be very similar to that of a question that is crying out to be answered. For example, if the other person talks about one of their hobbies and you talk about what you know about that activity by adding an opinion, the other person will feel called to position themselves before such affirmations.

Steps to Surviving an Awkward Conversation

Whether you're thinking about telling your coworker about the issue of personal hygiene, or if you have to face a dramatic situation in which someone needs to be comforted because something serious has happened, you are likely to feel pushed to remain silent.

It is natural since these types of conversations are usually really uncomfortable.

How to face an awkward interaction?

When there is an issue that inevitably slips away, and we are unable to articulate a discourse towards that person, discomfort and environmental tension may increase.

Once you are determined to face the situation, do not forget these tips that will help you to ensure that the pending conversation does not become a bad drink.

1. Avoid the silences

The investigations reveal that, after only four seconds of awkward silence, our anxiety levels soar. Also, the more anxious you feel, the more it will cost you to articulate the words.

To avoid this, you should, as far as possible, plan the interaction a little in advance. If you know what you want to communicate, your message will be clear and crisp, and you will save yourself the discomfort generated by a choppy conversation and with the dreaded silences.

2. Talk in an intimate place

It is not a good idea to have a relevant conversation in a busy place with distractions (people nearby, noises ...). Find a private place where you can feel relaxed and where there are no people who can hear you or intrude.

If it is the other person, who starts talking about that awkward topic before you, suggest that you find a comfortable place to discuss it in confidence and without outside interference.

3. Take a seat

When you have to talk about an uncomfortable topic, it is a good idea that we are resting on a sofa or chair. We will feel more comfortable, especially if the subject is thorny or can lead to a significant emotional shock.

When you sit next to (or in front of) the other person, try to be at the same height. If you stand and the other person is sitting, you will give an image of superiority that can be very negative for the good of the interaction.

4. Start with a touch of attention

Hard conversations can be equally incisive but better received if you use a touch of prior attention. For example, instead of saying: "Miguel, the other workers can't stand more than a minute near you," you can start with a phrase that softens the context, like: "Miguel, what I'm going to tell you can be a bit hard to fit in."

This nuance makes the other person have a few seconds to prepare mentally and emotionally for what you will tell him after a moment.

5. Accept your discomfort as normal

Attempting to deny the discomfort may cause the opposite effect as desired. We can still feel more uncomfortable with the situation we face. If you notice something shaky, restless, and are unable to maintain eye contact with your interlocutor ... accept that you are a little nervous.

It is highly recommended that, in such a situation, you can say a phrase that reveals the discomfort shared with the interlocutor. For example: "I feel a little uncomfortable talking about this." This will cause your interlocutor to empathize with you, and the level of discomfort is likely to fall.

6. Be polite but also direct

It is essential that you manage to express yourself with correctness and trying not to disrespect. This is a basic tip: you must be careful if you want your message to come to fruition. However, you can run the risk of softening your words to the limit, and this can generate a weak message that is not received with the necessary forcefulness from your interlocutor.

Therefore, it is interesting that you stick to the facts, use your assertiveness, and send a clear message without too many circumlocutions and going straight to the root of the matter.

7. Practice active listening

Communication is a matter of two. You must let your caller process the information you just sent him, calmly. To be a good listener, it is important that you be receptive when listening to the other person's response, trying to share the issue and trying to resolve some points or misunderstandings.

If what you just said is especially hard, you should be prepared for the other person to experience (and express) intense emotions. These can range from shame or sadness, to fear or anger. In any case, you should try to make the person feel that he has support in you, and give him some time to face the situation.

How to start a conversation with whoever you want

Relationship with others is something basic and fundamental to have a satisfying life, but it is not always easy. And, although it seems a lie, knowing how to start a conversation properly can become a problem, in certain situations, even for the most extroverted people.

Now, despite the fact that for many people, this means leaving the comfort zone, the art of starting to talk to whomever, we want is a skill that can be learned.

Learn to know how to start a conversation

Something as simple as knowing how to start a conversation spontaneously with someone we are interested in maybe what makes the difference between having a full social life or not having it. And there are people who are so afraid of such situations that they end up isolating themselves and having few friends, which in turn is a way of having a rather small social support network.

Below are some basics about how to start a conversation.

1. Learn to tolerate failure

The first thing you have to be clear about is that as much as you read, that will only help you know what strategies to follow to face this facet of your social life; It is impossible to learn these kinds of things without having gone into practice. And that means that, necessarily, we will have to go through somewhat awkward situations to achieve a medium and long-term goal much more beneficial than the slight discomfort that comes out of the comfort zone at the beginning.

There is no magic recipe that solves the issue overnight without having put effort into it. The key is knowing how to make that effort productive.

2. Don't be a perfectionist with the moment

Almost any site is good to start a conversation, as long as the other person is not in a hurry. Sometimes, the fact of stopping to analyze whether the context is conducive to approach someone and initiate a dialogue is nothing more than an excuse (masked under rationality) to let these opportunities pass.

3. In the beginning, choose questions

When you start practicing how to start conversations, the fact that you will probably feel nervous, and some anxiety will limit your range of action. Therefore, it is good to recognize this small obstacle and act accordingly. And one way to do it is to make the moment to start a dialogue brief for oneself, and longer for the other person. That is to say: what we will do is pass the responsibility of the dialogue to the other by means of a question that the interlocutor must answer.

Now, for this to work, that question must give way to an answer that is not short and has a relative complexity. In this way, we will avoid that what we get back is a simple phrase of few words, and an awkward silence appears. The objective is that the response of the other allows us to comment on what has been said, and make the dialogue drift towards something else. Once this has been done, it is easier to feel comfortable with the situation.

4. Start with the easy

This is one of the classic recommendations of psychology, and it really works. If we approach very ambitious goals at the beginning, we will most likely get frustrated and end up throwing in the towel. You have to educate yourself to see that starting a conversation does not trigger unwanted consequences, and for that, it is good to start with people we do not feel vulnerable too, despite being relatively unknown people.

5. Learn to listen

Paradoxically, what causes discomfort when starting a conversation with someone who imposes respect on us is not the fact of starting to speak, but what can happen right after, when we have to act again after having seen the reaction of the other. Therefore, it is very important to learn to listen.

If we listen to what the other person says, distancing ourselves from the situation and concentrating our attention on the content of their message, it is very easy for spontaneous reflections, questions, or appreciations to arise that may be interesting to share.

Given that while training basic social skills, our role cannot be very outgoing, it is good to adopt the role of someone who knows how to listen: everyone likes to feel that there is someone who pays attention to what is said.

6. Give the message-centered response

At this point, we should limit ourselves to answering about what the other person has said, although we can already introduce other related ideas or even personal experiences. Since the conversation has already been initiated, it can already drift in virtually any direction, provided that everything starts from the intervention of the other person.

How to communicate better with others?

Before seeing the specific techniques to apply in your social relationships to better connect with those around you, it is important to understand some basic principles of communication, whether in the field of friendship, partner, or work. They are the following.

1. You are responsible for making yourself understood

Does that old saying "I am responsible for what I say, not what you understand" sound to you? Well, you will be interested that this is false, or at least partially false. Communication does not work as a system for transmitting data packets that one broadcasts outwards, and that's it; It is something much more dynamic, we must participate in the process by which the other person interprets what we say.

This is because the simple fact of being a person different from the recipient already makes our point of view and experiences lived in the past and in the present different, which means that no matter how well we do it, misunderstandings can always appear.

2. You have to put yourself in the shoes of others

This advice is derived from the previous one since the communication process is something dynamic, and we must ensure that there are no errors.

3. The context must be taken into account

Beyond the individuals involved in the act of communication in the context and these conditions, both what is said and how what is said is interpreted that should always be considered a very important factor.

For example, it is not the same to say something in a meeting in a restaurant than in the office where you work and being one of the two the head of the company.

Techniques to express yourself better and connect with other people

Given the above, we can now see several tips on how to communicate better with others and make this improve your social relationships.

1. Adapt your language

It is very important to adapt the language to the conversation you are having, especially considering two factors: the training and educational level of those who listen, and the context in which the conversation occurs.

For example, if you dedicate yourself to biology research and want to explain what a breed of dog you have at home is like, you should definitely avoid using very technical jargon, unless the other person asks you to explain those details.

On the other hand, if you are in a professional context, it is likely that you will not see with good eyes that you express yourself as you would do with your lifelong friends; As much as this is an arbitrary imposition, failing to comply with these unwritten rules may overshadow the content of your message, in addition to wearing down your image in many cases.

2. Look in the eyes

This is possibly one of the simplest and at the same time, basic tips on how to communicate better. If you do not, a strange situation will be generated in which it will be difficult to interpret what you say, since your intentions will not be clear (since you will be talking but at the same time you show that you would like to be anywhere else except having that conversation).

Of course, so that you do not become obsessed with something so basic, it is better that you worry about not stop looking into the eyes for many seconds in a row, rather than focusing on looking all the time in the eyes. Ideally, do it with a spontaneity that allows you to forget about the matter unless you detect that you are not fulfilling it.

3. Avoid prejudging

Sometimes we may be tempted to express prejudices out loud about others, whether positive or negative, if only to generate conversation. Avoid this. In any case, ask questions to allow others to let themselves know more.

4. See if the other person feels nervous

Occasionally, you will encounter people prone to feeling nervous during conversations, especially if they know you very little.

By detecting these signs of stress, show them your complicity and use strategies to relieve tension and create a more relaxed environment: make a joke, adopt a relaxed nonverbal language, show that you take the other person seriously, and care what you think about you, etc.

5. Practice active listening

When they talk to you, don't adopt a passive attitude. Although it is your turn to remain silent, it shows that you are paying attention: look in the eyes, nod, react with some exclamations depending on the emotions caused by what you hear , and occasionally, add small comments or ask questions related to the subject (as long as they don't involve telling a story that is too long that doesn't matter too much in that situation). This is what is known as active listening.

CHAPTER SIX
The Importance of Social Skills to Achieve Objectives

Social skills are attitudes that drive relationships with others in an effective and healthy way. A person with these characteristics will know how to deal with any group with whom they should interact, fostering a harmonious environment, focused on solving problems and achieving goals together.

Despite the automation of tasks, efficient human interaction is required to streamline workflows, and today, more than ever, customer experience is an essential element for the development of a company, a close and humane treatment is required that No machine could generate.

Good teamwork translates into productivity, and companies know it, for this reason, In addition to well-trained professionals, they require among their ranks people with well-developed social skills, who are able to provide cohesion to the team to achieve objectives.

What characteristics does a person with social skills have?

Being outgoing does not necessarily mean that you have social skills; you can simply be narcissistic, so focused on yourself that any possibility of assertive communication is blocked. Someone with true skills has:

Communication ability

Having communication skills implies knowing how to listen to the interlocutor. In addition to understanding what he says in words, knowing how to read the nonverbal language. A person who knows how to communicate is able to adapt the language, gestures, and tone of voice according to the interlocutor and according to what you want to get from the talk.

Leadership

Being able to delegate, motivate, convey confidence, and set goals among your team. A person with social skills knows how to make their partners feel good, gives them their place, and considers each achievement as the result of a joint effort.

Resilience

He is someone who does not give up and is able to face crises and setbacks with a good attitude. A resilient person sees problems as an opportunity to prove himself.

Flexibility

In a changing world, the ability to adapt and not be afraid to face the unknown is an important attribute. This quality allows being open to new ideas, favoring creativity and innovation, and is an indispensable element when negotiating.

How can these skills be enhanced to succeed in achieving goals?

While it is true that there are those who have a temperament that favors these qualities, it is also true that any type of skill is susceptible to learning and is perfected with practice.

Communication

Practice at home with body gestures, facial expression, tone of voice, perform vocalization exercises. Adopting an upright posture not only makes you look better before others but also before yourself.

Learn to listen. When you talk to someone, actively listen to what they are saying instead of thinking about what you are going to answer.

Don't deny your emotions

Accept your emotions, even negative ones such as anxiety or fear, but don't wait to feel safe to act. This brings us to the next point:

Take the initiative

Dare to expose your views. Do not wait to be told what to do. If you are introverted, every day, set a small challenge that will help you get out of your comfort zone to interact with others. Use emotional communication to generate empathy.

CHAPTER SEVEN
Self-Discipline

Self-discipline is the ability to follow the rules imposed personally, with order and constancy, using only willpower.

Self-discipline is a virtue that is acquired with constancy. Being a disciplined person means focusing on the goals you want to achieve, whether in the personal, work, or academic field.

The ability to self-discipline requires the transformation of the discipline into the habit, respecting the rules and norms imposed by each one until it becomes normal.

The Importance of Self-Discipline.
If we want to create a new habit or routine, we need to perform the actions we want until they have become natural, that is, until we have developed self-discipline.

However, before explaining to you how we can develop it, there is something else that is fundamental to understand.

Self-discipline is not a once-developed skill that is stored in a drawer in the brain, ready to use when you feel like it.

If you are going to start developing your self-discipline, you have to do it on a regular basis, ideally every day or every two days. Although it can be developed gradually, it has to be done consistently.

How to develop self-discipline.

1- Define precisely what to do.

If you want to develop self-discipline, you have to know what you need it for. Whether it is tidying up, playing an instrument, reading, studying, going to the gym, or anything else you want to do, but you are not getting it, the important thing is to know what you want.

Although it sounds basic, many people say they want to have more self-discipline but are not sure what they want to do with it, or at best give too abstract answers such as "I want to have the self-discipline to be more productive."

That will be very difficult! It is essential to be as specific as possible about what you want.

2- Know when you will do it.

If you do not plan ahead what action you need to take, something will get in the way, you will miss the time you thought was the best, and you will continue to apologize to yourself as "an unexpected has arisen. Suddenly"or"I haven't had time yet."

3- Know how long you will perform the intended action.

And this is where the magic happens! If you don't have self-discipline, you should start by setting mini-goals.

Mini goals are realistic goals given your particular situation. They should not cause too much discomfort, and you must be absolutely sure that you can do them.

For example, let's say you want more self-discipline to use 1 hour every two days to tidy up the house.

Starting with 1 hour, maybe too much. Even the thought of having to clean the house for an hour every two days can cause unbearable anxiety that doesn't even start.

Self-Discipline to Achieve Your Goals

Everyone knows the word "discipline." At its mere evocation, it produces strange reactions, ranging from fear to disgust, to hatred. After all, who wants to be "stupid and disciplined"? Discipline would then be only a kind of rigid framework reserved for the military and other trades subject to an uncompromising hierarchy.

That said, there is another way of looking at discipline, and more specifically, self-discipline. Although there are many qualities to cultivate that can contribute to our achievements and make us happy, only self-discipline allows us to achieve lasting success in our lives.

Whether it's about eating, our physical condition, our work or our relationships, self-discipline is crucial to achieving our goals, leading a healthy lifestyle, and ultimately being happy. It is at the base of the habits that are put in place in our life. Without it, we lose our sense of organization and our priorities.

To summarize, self-discipline allows us to continue this activity to the end, or to practice this new habit continuously. But cultivating self-discipline also requires having an intrinsic motivation, an irresistible reason that drives us to keep moving forward. And each time we think back to that reason, we find meaning in our actions.

Moreover, contrary to what many people think, self-discipline is a learned behavior. It requires practicing and repeating it daily. So, to develop your self-discipline and improve your life here is 5 essential steps to take:

- **You need a good reason**

You want to do something important to you. Maybe to get back to sports, or to eat better, or to stop smoking? That's fine, but your desire is not enough. You need a reason, or better, several important reasons to get started.

Without a strong desire, you have little chance of developing your self-discipline. Autodisicipline requires fuel to work, and that fuel is your motivation. Otherwise, you will not be able to focus or stay consistent with achieving your goal.

If you miss the reasons, it's time to ask yourself some questions:

- What would I like to do, be, or accomplish? What habits would I like to develop? Or what behavior would I like to change?
- What am I trying to accomplish by doing X (this task /behavior/habit)?
- Why do I want to do X (this task /behavior/ habit)?
- What do I need to be able to be consistent in X (this task /behavior/ habit)?

The more reasons you identify for your task or habit, the more energy you will have to grow your self-discipline. But that's not all…

- **You must commit**

It is not enough to have good reasons to adopt a new behavior or to perform an activity. You must also make a firm commitment to do whatever it takes to reach your goal.

Of course, it's not easy. Long-term commitment takes a lot of effort, and not many people do it on their own. What they lack is a responsibility.

To continue to perform a habit or action, we must be responsible for our actions. Being responsible means that you will assume your failures and your successes; you will not be able to blame anyone but you.

Being engaged also means overcoming the challenges you face, organizing yourself so that other tasks or individuals do not come to disturb you. Of course, it's easier said than done. The important thing is that you stay constant. If you fail to do so, assume that failure and immediately reattempt another time to commit to doing it seriously.

For this, it is necessary to create a number of guidelines:

- What standards will I follow when I perform X (when / where / how / with whom)?
- What behaviors and habits should I cultivate to accomplish this goal?
- What behaviors and choices should I refuse for me? What obstacles will I face?
- How can I rectify things if I make a bad movie?

To put the odds on your side, it is also necessary to limit distractions.

- **Limit distractions**

By removing all temptations and distractions from your environment, you will facilitate the implementation of your new behavior /habit/activity. If you want to better manage the food you eat and then throw away all the junk food that hangs in your closets. Politely refuse invitations to restaurants that do not offer healthy dishes.

If you want to improve your concentration at work, then turn off your laptop and unclutter your desktop. If your activity is computer-related and you find it hard not to fall in social networks and other distractions, then download the Self-control app and program it to filter your favorite websites during the time that you wish.

Only by eliminating all these bad influences will you succeed in doing what you want.

On the other hand, you can also create a work environment that will allow you to be more motivated. Add motivating phrases or even a viewing board. Do not hesitate to build your own ritual in which you will perform the same actions in the same place at the same time.

By having a particular setting, you do not need to think about acting. Everything comes naturally to you. Just sitting on that office chair at this exact time triggers your work behavior.

- **Write an action plan**

When it comes to developing self-discipline, it's important to have a clear vision of what you are trying to accomplish. To understand your own definition of success. After all, if you do not know where you are going, then it's easy to get lost on the way or be distracted.

With a clear plan that outlines all the steps you will take to reach your goals, you will stay focused on what you have to do. It's not for nothing that you have a 42% chance of achieving your goals when you score them. Just visualizing what you have to do will allow you to program your mind to succeed.

Just start, divide your goal into a number of small, easy-to-do tasks. Instead of changing everything overnight or going up to 1000% in your new habit, take the time to take a step after another. If you are looking to get fit, then start exercising 10 to 15 minutes a day. Or if you want to sleep better, try to go to bed 15 minutes earlier each night.

There are no small achievements, only bricks that will pave the way towards your goal. Once you are comfortable with what you are already doing, you will be able to increase the difficulty or duration of your habits/behaviors/ tasks.

Do not forget to prepare a backup plan. If you are looking for healthy eating and at the last moment you are invited to a family dinner where sweet and fatty products are served, take a little time to stop. Tell yourself that instead of diving into the aperitifs, you will sip a glass of water and concentrate on the discussions.

With a plan in mind, you have the right mindset to handle any situation. You also save energy by not having to make hasty decisions based on your emotions.

- **Follow your progress**

A self-disciplined spirit flourishes when he recognizes the progress he is making towards a goal. That's why it's important to note your progress, with a calendar or diary.

This will help you measure what you have accomplished and what remains to be done, which will allow you to stay motivated and focused on your tasks. In addition, even in situations where you fail, tracking your progress will allow you to make the necessary adjustments to keep moving forward.

When it comes to tracking your progress, it is necessary to monitor your results as well as the temptations that ultimately sabotage your progress. Once identified, make the necessary adjustments to avoid these temptations.

Remember that very rarely things will run smoothly. There will always be pitfalls to go through, challenges to overcome. It's part of life. Nevertheless, with self-discipline, you will overcome these obstacles.

When things are not going to be the same as you've decided, you'll have to apologize and complain through the window. Apologies and complaints never solve anything, it's even the opposite. Mastering your emotions becomes an important skill for cultivating your self-discipline. When your emotions are on your side, they help you find the strength to continue making efforts to reach your goal.

CHAPTER EIGHT
Make an excellent impression

Making an excellent first impression in a job interview is essential to stand out from the rest of the candidates. Learn how to proceed.

The first impression made is central to a job interview. Can one be misleading and limit one's knowledge about someone? Yes, it can; it is a fact. But if you really want to be the one for the job you are applying for, you have to do your best to get the best first impression possible right away.

To do this, there are several points to consider in order to successfully move to the first selection of candidates and stand out from the start. Do not neglect and surprise the interviewer for the positive!

What Can You Do To Make An Excellent First Impression?

1. Give the first impression the due importance

Studies say that 30 seconds is the time it takes the brain to form a first impression. Thus, with the first glance he puts on himself, the recruiter immediately forms the first impression - which is based on what his immediate appearance conveys to him.

2. Wear proper dress code and care

When you go to a job interview, you have to pay close attention to the clothes you wear, as the image is key. In fact, it really conveys the value we place on that interview and the effort we put into it. Do not, therefore, give a sloppy air to your physical appearance. Wear the proper dress code and go with a careful physical appearance

3. Learn to speak and listen

At first glance, presenting good language performance is critical. The recruiter will not pass to a second phase a candidate who does not know what he says or how he says, who does not reveal a coherent speech and in careful language. At the same time, knowing how to listen is also important. Don't talk nonstop or interrupt your interviewer. Know, therefore, when to speak and when to listen.

4. Show security

Although you may have insecurities, do not reveal them. Show yourself safe, confident, smiling, and maintain direct eye contact with the interviewer. It is also convenient to incorporate your safety. Prepare conveniently before the interview.

5. Be humble

At first glance, humility is key. Therefore, having an arrogant posture will certainly not take you to a good end. So be willing to learn and be simple and friendly.

6. Have a correct posture

Do not forget the manners! Greet everyone equally. If you know the name, use it when addressing the person. Have a firm handshake, and always be polite and respectful. Also, learn how to sit down and not be too relaxed, as you may pass a sloppy image that is certainly not what you want to convey.

7. Be professional

Be punctual. Arriving late for an interview is not synonymous with a good first impression. In fact, it may well mean the end of the meeting, even before it started. Do not blame others for what has done less well in the projects you have been to, nor take full credit for their success. Talk about your mistakes and successes as naturally.

8. Show yourself available

Do not start from the beginning to put obstacles. Show yourself available for teamwork and learning. Having good openness is essential!

CHAPTER NINE
Anxiety

Anxiety is a feeling that is difficult to clearly define. Each of us may come into contact with it, because internal anxiety may appear both in the case of various temporary, difficult life situations and in connection with mental disorders. So how do you get rid of the feeling of internal anxiety, what are the causes of anxiety, and why do we still feel internal anxiety?

We have all felt anxiety at some point: before an exam, a job interview, a public exhibition, but when it is installed in our lives beginning to limit our day today.

After a breakup, a loss of a loved one or just suddenly, for no apparent reason, is when anxiety begins to worry us.

What is anxiety?

Anxiety is an adaptive response of the human being, provided that it is proportionate to the stimulus that triggers it. It is an alarm signal that if it continues over time for no apparent reason, it is telling us that we have something to review in our lives.

Another positive aspect of anxiety is its relationship with performance, described in the Yertes-Dobson Act in 1908; This law states that when faced with a stressful situation, such as taking an exam, anxiety increases, but there is also an increase in efficiency, attention, and performance in the response, as long as it does not go beyond limits. If we exceed that line, then the performance drops and the information retrieval processes are blocked.

Anxiety begins to worry us when it appears suddenly, unjustifiably, and for no apparent reason. If the physical symptoms are very high, we will also be scared. Tachycardia, shortness of breath, dizziness, muscle tension, etc., are some of the characteristic symptoms of anxiety. When its appearance is maintained over time, in a high way and before stimuli that do not pose a real threat, it is when we talk about maladaptive anxiety.

When anxiety manifests itself without prior warning or apparent reason, it can generate a decrease in self-esteem and the "fear of going crazy" typical of anxiety; this, in turn, generates a lowered mood and a feeling of helplessness.

Sometimes, stress, the appearance of specific problems or difficulties, a traumatic event, or the loss of a loved one, are some of the causes that are behind anxiety.

Examples of anxiety disorders

This disproportionate anxiety results in different manifestations or pictures of anxiety, such as:

- Generalized Anxiety Disorder (GAD).
- Anxiety crisis.
- Panic.
- Agoraphobia.

Main symptoms

Next, we will see the physical symptoms, that is, the physiological reactions on our body; cognitive symptoms, related to cognitions, thoughts, and effects on information processing; and the symptoms related to behavior and how anxiety influences it.

- **Physical symptoms of anxiety**

These are the main physical symptoms of anxiety.

- Tachycardia.
- The sensation of pressure in the chest and that breath is missing.
- Muscle tension and tremors.
- Cold sweats.
- Tingling in limbs, sensations of pressed skin.
- Difficulty falling asleep or waking up startled in the middle of the night.
- Lack of appetite or overeating and without hunger.
- stress or knot in the stomach.
- Feeling dizzy, etc.

- **Cognitive symptoms**

Among the cognitive symptoms of anxiety, we highlight the following.

- Excessively negative or catastrophic thoughts.

- Recurring thoughts of fear of the appearance of physical symptoms, anticipating them.
- Thoughts of anticipation of the future, with fear of becoming and uncertainty.
- Difficulty in maintaining attention and concentration, significantly lowering memory capacity
- Disorientation and feeling of loss of control.
- Fear of going crazy.

- **Behavioral symptoms of anxiety**

Finally, these are the symptoms that are planted in actions.

- Busy sites or leaving home alone are avoided.
- Social relationships can be avoided.
- Constantly check to have a sense of control, whether about the future for fear of uncertainty, fear of illness, etc. It is usually done by asking family and friends, devising the doctor more than usual, etc.
- Constantly check that everything is in order, to feel some control.

Treatment with a psychologist: how is it done?

The psychologist is aware of how limiting anxiety is for their patients when they do not understand how anxiety works. The good news is that understanding and knowing what it is is the first step to overcome it.

Many people suffer the appearance of symptoms without warning and suddenly, which causes them to spend most of their time on alert. This alert is what ends up generating before or after the onset of symptoms. This unpredictability about the appearance of anxiety crises is one of the causes that most impact on the person since it can generate low moods.

The success of cognitive-behavioral therapy in the treatment of anxiety disorders is evident ; Today, it is very positive results in its treatment are more than known thanks to the application of techniques developed after long years of research in psychology, such as progressive exposure techniques, systematic desensitization and the development of coping and de-learning skills of anxiety

During therapy, a fundamental objective is for the person to learn to use these techniques in their day-to-day life and thus recover the feeling of control over their body and their mood so that they can remit the symptoms of anxiety and its crises.

Along with the anxiety de-learning techniques of cognitive-behavioral psychology, the work in psychotherapy of emotions through humanistic psychology as well as the latest techniques developed from the discoveries of Neuropsychology, such as EMDR or Brain Integration Techniques.

For the psychologist, the main objective is not that anxiety disappears, but that the person loses fear of anxiety and its appearance: by identifying how anxiety manifests in our body, emotion and thought and being aware that it is a sign of alarm that can teach us a lot about ourselves and how to improve our lives.

Types of Anxiety (Characteristics, Causes, and Symptoms)

We have all felt anxiety from time to time. It is a normal emotion. It is possible that, just before an exam, because of a work problem or because you needed to make an important decision, you experienced its symptoms.

This occurs because anxiety is a normal reaction of people in situations of stress and uncertainty. The problem arises when several anxious symptoms cause distress or some degree of functional deterioration in the life of the individual who suffers it because it affects the functioning in different areas of his life. For example, social and family relationships, work, school.

Anxiety disorders: a very common pathology

The anxiety disorder is one of the most common diseases. Now, with proper treatment, people who suffer from it can learn to manage their symptoms and improve their quality of life.

Since there are notable differences between the different types of anxiety disorders, we explain the different types of anxiety:

1. Generalized anxiety disorder

Many individuals feel anxious or worried from time to time, especially when they have to face situations that can be stressful: public speaking, playing a football game that means a lot, or going to a job interview. This type of anxiety can make you alert, helping you to be more productive, and to do the job more efficiently.

People who suffer from generalized anxiety disorder (ADD), however, feel anxiety and worry most of the time, not just in potentially stressful situations. These concerns are intense, irrational, persistent (at least half of the days for at least 6 months), and interfere with normal functioning in your daily life (activities such as work, school, friends, and family), as they are difficult to control.

2. Panic Disorder

The panic disorder is an anxiety disorder very debilitating and different TAD. While the generalized anxiety disorder is known as trait anxiety, as it is more lasting, the panic disorder is known as anxiety state, since its symptomatology is acute.

People with panic disorder experience feelings of death or the possibility of running out of the air, which can cause both psychological and physical problems. In fact, the sensation can be so intense that it requires hospitalization.

In summary, the panic attack is characterized by:

- The presence of recurring and unexpected panic attacks
- Concern after having had a panic attack that another will happen, at least for a month.
- Concern about the implications or consequences of a panic attack (such as thinking that a panic attack is a sign of an undiagnosed medical problem). For example, some people have repeated medical tests because of these concerns and, despite the negative test results, they still have fears of discomfort.
- Significant changes in behavior that are related to panic attacks (such as avoiding activities such as physical exercise, like heart rate increases).

3. Obsessive-Compulsive Disorder

Anxious thoughts can influence our behavior, which can be positive sometimes. For example, thinking that you may have left the oven on may cause you to check it out. However, if such thoughts are recurring, it can lead an individual to carry out unhealthy behaviors.

Obsessive-Compulsive Disorder (OCD) is characterized in that the individual sufferer has thoughts, ideas, or intrusive images. These cause anxiety (obsessions) and cause the person to perform certain rituals or actions (compulsions) to reduce discomfort.

Some examples of obsessive thoughts are fear of contamination or feeling of doubt (for example, will I have closed the door of the house?), among others. Compulsions are, for example, wash your hands, repeatedly check that the door is closed, count, and repeatedly organize things, and so on.

4. Post-traumatic Stress Disorder (PTSD)

This condition occurs when the person has experienced a traumatic situation that has caused great psychological stress, which can be disabling. When the person relives the fact that the trauma caused him, he may experience the following symptoms: nightmares, feelings of anger, irritability or emotional fatigue, detachment from others, and so on.

Due to the great anxiety that the individual feels. He can try to avoid situations or activities that remind him of the event that caused the trauma.

5. Social phobia

Social phobia is characterized by an irrational fear of situations of social interaction. For example, individuals who suffer from this type of anxiety disorder feel disabling anxiety when they have to speak in public because they are afraid of being judged, criticized, humiliated, and think that others will laugh at them in front of others. Social phobia is a serious disorder, and some individuals may even suffer from talking on the phone or eating in front of other people.

6. Agoraphobia

The agoraphobia usually associated with the irrational fear of being in open spaces and large streets or parks. Actually, the agoraphobic feels strong anguish caused by situations where he feels unprotected and vulnerable to anxiety crises beyond his control. Therefore, fear is not produced by these spaces in themselves, but by the consequences of being exposed to that place, where they feel helpless. This means that in the most serious cases, the patient can be confined to his home as a form of avoidance.

7. Specific phobia

A specific phobia is an anxiety disorder that is characterized by a strong, irrational fear of a stimulus, for example, a situation, an object, a place, or an insect. The person who suffers from a phobic disorder does everything possible to avoid this stimulus that causes anxiety, and this avoidant behavior can interfere with the normal functioning of his daily life.

CHAPTER TEN
The keys to overcoming anxiety

Anxiety can manifest itself in different ways but with the same emotional state: the feeling of threat and danger coupled with the feeling of helplessness and vulnerability.

The threat can come, in the most ordinary cases, from habitual problems in our life, such as fear of infidelity or breakup in the couple, of not being able to pass an exam, of not doing a job well, of not getting an acceptance or social approval, etc.

In disorders treated by psychologists the threat has a more irrational and less realistic character, it can occur in panic attacks as fear of a heart attack, in hypochondria it can be fear of contracting cancer or AIDS, in phobia social is the fear of criticism or ridicule, in generalized anxiety can be the fear that a family member has an accident or in obsessive disorder may be the fear of pollution.

Either the anxiety for problems of living or psychological disorders, in both cases, the experience of inability to control or face a threat accompanies it. In clinical cases, the feeling of helplessness and vulnerability is much more intense.

If you are currently experiencing anxiety, you should read the following clues to be able to face it and overcome it. If you have any type of treatment, you can consult with your psychologist or therapist the application of the following keys.

key 1: learn to change negative thoughts.

The negative thoughts can be very varied, but they usually pick up the central fear of the person: "Surely they suspend me", "The plane will have a breakdown, and it will crash", "It will give me a heart attack", " My son has had an accident", "If I don't give the switch a great misfortune will happen", " I'm sure I keep my mind blank and make the most terrible ridicule ".

Insistently thinking about something negative generates the activation of the organism's alarm system that puts itself in a position to face danger; for example, the heart beats faster, preparing the confrontation or escapes response. Therefore, it is essential to learn to change negative thoughts. This goal is usually one of the most important in the work of psychologists, not only for the treatment of anxiety but for any other type of emotional disorder.

The mechanics of changing thoughts consist of learning to identify negative thoughts that are usually quite automatic and, therefore, unconscious. A person can immerse themselves in dialogues and negative thoughts without having a clear awareness of being "hypnotized" by the tyranny of thoughts.

In order to raise awareness, we have to write them, if possible, at the same moment when they occur, if we cannot at that time, we will do so as soon as we can.

Subsequently, we must strive to write rational and realistic thoughts as an antidote to toxic negative thoughts. It is a literary exercise that is doing that as we can learn a language, our mind is learning to rectify and change by encouraging more realistic and positive thoughts in our usual way of thinking.

It is convenient to read over and over again, realistic and positive thoughts. It is possible that although with the rational mind, we believe that they are true, with our hearts we still do not believe it.

key 2: learn to change the fight against anxiety by accepting it.

Psychologists call primary anxiety to the one caused by life's own problems, such as work, partner or children, economy, health, etc ... but when a person's fear is directed towards one's anxiety, we have secondary anxiety. That is, a person is scared to experience fear or anxiety.

And of course, in secondary anxiety it is about avoiding everything that causes anxiety : in the case of panic attacks, physical sensations that are associated with serious diseases are avoided, such as noticing the heartbeat, in the case of social phobia, social situations that generate anxiety are avoided, in the case of obsessive disorders, negative thoughts that generate anxiety are avoided, in agoraphobia, the street or closed places with difficult exit, etc.

Well, it is something well known by psychologists how fighting anxiety or avoiding situations that cause it generates more anxiety. The person with anxiety tries not to perceive in his body the angiogenic sensations and not go to places where anxiety can be triggered.

Therefore, being able to overcome anxiety paradoxically requires an attitude of acceptance, of "surrender" and does not fight against the manifestations of anxiety. It is convenient that one dares to feel the manifestations of anxiety in the body fully, paying attention, and not judging the symptoms of anxiety as good or bad. They are simply sensations that we have to get used to.

key 3: Face your fears.

Even if you change your thoughts and get a good level of acceptance of feelings of anxiety, you will not be able to overcome anxiety until you face everything that frightens you, and you can overcome it.

If you are afraid of the relationship with people, you will have to expose yourself, even gradually, to social situations. If you are afraid to touch things that may contaminate you, you will have to do so. If your fear has to do with being in closed situations, you will have to gradually expose yourself until your anxiety level decreases in these situations. If your fears have to do with unreal situations as an accident happens to a loved one, you will have to imagine it repeatedly until this fear diminishes.

Psychologists used to prepare a scale of situations from less to greater anxiety to gradually generate training in overcoming fear. For example, if your fear is agoraphobic, and you are afraid to go out alone for fear that you have an anxiety crisis and have no one who can help you, a list is made starting with the situation that least fear you cause, for example, to go out to the door of the street, continue distancing myself a few meters, reach the corner, turn around the block, walk 3 minutes away from the house, 5 minutes, etc.

The cognitive-behavioral treatment administered by psychologists to overcome anxiety

Anxiety therapy is very varied, depending on the type of disorder being treated. But these three keys are usually present in one way or another in all treatments. Exposure is a fundamental part of overcoming anxiety since only when you show yourself that you are able to face situations, you can have the security and confidence necessary to feel good. You have to insist on the exposures as long as you need until the anxiety levels are non-existent, and the negative thoughts of threat and danger are not generated.

The emotional acceptance of anxiety is a very important section since it implies an important change of the person that implies an increase in tolerance to negative emotional ones and with it an increase in the quality of life.

Anxiety as a sign of intelligence

In our day today, it is quite common to feel stressed or anxious. We carry out tasks too quickly, while we don't want to stop to understand our surroundings. We need to get to the point we have in mind without much delay, and we let loose ends along the way because of it, worrying excessively...

In those moments, surely, your environment keeps telling you that you need to stop and enjoy it. They may even suggest that you have an anxiety problem because you are not carrying it out and need support to overcome it.

It is true that to enjoy a healthy and balanced quality of life, we need to stop and allow ourselves to enjoy, but today I will tell you that those moments in which you worry and feel anxiety can also be signs of high intelligence. Without forgetting in the latter obviously, healthy management of them.

These data that corroborate high levels of intelligence in relation to anxiety have been extracted from research published in Science Direct, providing a new report on human intelligence such as the one I will share with you below.

Anxiety implies greater linguistic intelligence

The research published in Science Direct studied the relationships between generalized anxiety disorder, depression, worry, and emotional management that take place after the experience, with the levels of linguistic and non-linguistic intelligence, using a sample of 126 people.

The data obtained indicated that verbal intelligence is related to anxiety disorder and depression symptoms positively. In this way, it was extracted that people who suffer from anxiety disorder and retain depressive symptoms show high levels of linguistic intelligence.

The link between anxiety and intelligence

It should be noted that in numerous previous studies and research, the existence of a relationship between anxiety and intelligence had already been proven. On this occasion, Lakehead psychologists have carried out a much broader study of the subject, obtaining as a conclusion that people who tend to worry at higher levels are much smarter.

Also, with the data obtained, it was confirmed that verbal intelligence, in this case, proved to be a perfect predictor of the levels of concern and intensity of emotional concern. With this, we can say that people who have higher levels of linguistic intelligence suffer higher levels of concern and develop anxiety disorders and depression more frequently.

In parallel, Jeremy Coplan in 2011 conducted a study confirming that high levels of concern in patients with a generalized anxiety disorder are positively related to the level of intelligence extracted by IC. On the other hand, there is also a positive relationship with the level of intelligence in people with low levels of concern, which do not suffer from a generalized anxiety disorder.

In conclusion, we can extract that both investigations confirm an intense relationship between intelligence and anxiety, confirming that those people who have been able to develop greater skills and talents are more likely to suffer psychological disorders.

CHAPTER ELEVEN
Relaxation Techniques to Anxiety

There are currently a number of methods and techniques that can generously assist the process of silencing the mind and calming daily agitation. Meditation, exercise, healthy eating, music therapy, and even natural remedies are excellent resources when it comes to relaxing and even getting quality sleep.

Daily restlessness and stress, as well as affecting one's mind, can cause muscle tension, thinning hair, dizziness, and headache, no matter who you are or how old you are. It is, therefore, crucial that people seek to relax whenever possible to prevent symptoms such as these or the aggravation of any existing psychological disorder.

There are some techniques recommended by experts that are not intended for drug treatment, and they are more natural practices that aim to just reduce stress, calm the mind and lessen the agitation experienced by people suffering from Anxiety Disorders. Are they:

Meditation: This technique can be applied to anyone at any time. During your practice, concentration tends to increase, dispelling confusing thoughts that may give rise to your discomfort. And there are several types of meditation, among the best known we can highlight:

Guided Meditation: In this type of meditation, mental images of relaxing places and situations are formed. In this technique, it is possible to stimulate many of our senses through smells, sounds, images, and textures.

Mantra: In this type of meditation, people repeat the same word or phrase or thought so that this repetition generates inner peace, balance, and focus.

Mindfulness: In this type of meditation, one becomes aware of the importance of living in the present moment, in the here and now. And though some kind of thinking comes to mind, it just lets it pass.

Qi Gong: To restore and maintain balance, this technique usually combines meditation with relaxation, physical movement, and breathing.

Tai Chi: This is a type of meditation that mixes with Chinese martial arts, where slow movements and postures are taken while breathing deeply.

Yoga: In this type of meditation, postures and breathing exercises are performed, accompanied by relaxing music as a sound resource. As the person performs the movements, they work their balance, focus, and stay more connected to the present moment.

Physical Exercises: Practicing at least 30 minutes of daily physical exercise has considerable benefits for the individual's emotions. This is a great time to think about solutions to everyday challenges. In addition, exercise helps eliminate cortisol (a stress hormone) and increases endorphin production, which aims to promote well-being.

Positive Thoughts: The fluctuation of our positive and negative perceptions can greatly affect our health and well-being, so we must always remain positive. In order not to fall into the trap of negativity, we can:

- Identify and change negative thoughts ;
- Identify which areas of life are most affected by pessimism;
- Seek to live with positive people;
- Evaluate rationally every negative thought that arises;
- Practice Gratitude daily;
- Seek to maintain a good mood even in the face of difficult times.

Time for You: There are people who can't say "no," even if they are exhausted and out of time, but saying "yes" to everything can cause even more stress. That's why it's important to take time to do things for yourself, something you enjoy, such as reading a book or cycling, walking in a park or being with family. Striking a balance between personal and professional life is essential for Anxiety and Stress to be kept under control.

Social Life: Hanging out with friends and being with family members greatly helps in reducing stress and anxiety. So taking a coffee break with friends in or out of the workplace, talking to family members, or phoning an acquaintance you haven't seen in a long time are all ways to relax while cultivating relationships and inner peace.

Healthy Eating: Eating in a balanced way, preferring foods rich in vitamin C, B5, B6, magnesium, and zinc over foods that overload and accelerate the body, such as caffeine, sugars, and alcohol, makes a huge difference in good. -Daily of people who have anxiety and stress disorder. Invest in strawberries, oranges, broccoli, eggs, fish, bananas, beans, almonds, corn, and peas among others.

Essential Oils and Massages: Combining these two techniques can truly bring the anxious and stressed person more peace, relaxation, and a sense of well-being. Lavender, Chamomile, or Eucalyptus essential oil massages are great for relieving muscle tension and stress symptoms that when left untreated can lead to an Anxiety Disorder.

CHAPTER TWELVE
Exercises to Overcome Stress and Improve Your Mental Health

There are so many things that occupy our mind that sometimes we lose our balance and get carried away by stress, we become somewhat anxious, depressed or irritable, and we stop enjoying those little things in life because of the tension generated by our day. a day.

There are some exercises to improve your mental health by overcoming stress and anxiety and achieve that balance we want so much, so don't worry anymore and put these tips into practice so you can make your day a better day.

1. Practice breathing techniques

A deep and conscious breath can allow you to overcome anxiety in just a few minutes because by decreasing heart rate and blood pressure, stress levels also decrease.

Try this breathing technique: take a moment of your time to get away from everything and focus on yourself; in a place where you feel comfortable, whether you're sitting or lying down, close your eyes and inhale through your nose while counting to four, then exhale through your nose, counting to four again; Repeat this sequence as many times as possible, until you feel completely relaxed.

Another exercise you can do while maintaining a deep and slow breath is progressive relaxation: tense and relax your muscles for a few seconds, starting with the feet until you reach the neck, jaw, and eyes, which will help you release tension from the feet to the head and will allow you to relax even more.

2. Put meditation into practice

Meditating for a few minutes a day in the comfort of your home or in any other space you like can help you overcome anxiety, increase your creativity, and achieve mental clarity and emotional stability.

To meditate, start by sitting straight with both feet on the floor and close your eyes, then concentrate on reciting, loudly or silently, some positive mantra or phrase, such as: "I love myself" "I give thanks for my life " I am a wonderful being. " Place one of your hands on your belly to synchronize your breathing with the mantra or prayer, and let all negative thoughts leave your mind.

This exercise will have greater benefits if you use breathing techniques such as the one explained above, or actively participate in guided meditations or yoga exercises for beginners. By joining a yoga group, you can acquire these benefits, remember that the practice of yoga is meditation in motion and allows you to increase your concentration.

3. Perform physical exercise

The exercise not only helps us to stay fit but also allows the oxygenation of the brain and reduced stress as it promotes the release of endorphins that give us that sense of well - being.

An easy and effective way to clear your mind is to do some exercise of your choice, it can be yoga or taichí, or any other that you find attractive, the important thing is that you do it with dedication and always taking into account that you do it for yourself, To see you and feel good.

4. Connect with nature

Going to the beach, a lake, a mountain, or a park and contemplating nature, can help you disperse that lot of things that go around in your head and that do not allow you to be yourself. Go to a place of your liking where you can see the plants, perceive their aroma, feel the breeze and breathe.

Dedicate a space of your time to connect with the beauty of the surroundings and that beauty will be reflected in you.

5. Practice visualization

In a place you like, close your eyes and visualize happy scenes, what you like, what you want to be or do; This activity will allow you to connect with what you so long for and it will make you feel that it is already part of you, so that you will feel much happier and can leave behind all that overwhelms you.

6. Laugh out loud

In addition to helping us reduce mental load, laughter helps us reduce depression, overcome anxiety and stress by lowering cortisol levels in the body and releasing endorphins that favor mood.

Surround yourself with positive people who make you laugh every day or devote yourself to watching comedy in your spare time, are some of the things you can do to laugh at least a little every day.

7. Connect with other people

Spend a little of your time getting in touch with other people and entertaining yourself; It does not matter if you use your social networks, telephone a friend or are in a place to enjoy a coffee and chat for a while, the important thing is that you can clear your mind and spend quality time with someone other than yourself.

8. Listen to the music you like

If you want to improve your mental health, one of the best ways to achieve this is by listening to soft music, as it helps decrease heart rate, blood pressure, and body anxiety, helping to achieve a state of mental tranquility.

9. Do what you like so much

Practice your favorite activities, and this will help you clear your mind and forget about everyday problems. Whether shopping, playing sports, swimming, watching a movie, or just going for ice cream, it will help you get out of the routine and feel happy with yourself for doing what is so pleasing.

10. Get enough sleep

When we do not sleep the necessary time, our body and our mind feel exhausted, so doing our daily activities is a somewhat difficult task to handle because we feel irritable, annoyed and have a hard time concentrating on what we should do.

Getting enough sleep will allow your body to replenish the energies it has spent, and upon waking, you will feel a sense of well-being that will allow you to start the day with the right foot.

CHAPTER THIRTEEN
Foods That Help Fight Anxiety

1. Bitter chocolate

Dark chocolate, the one with at least 70% cocoa in its composition, is a great food to reduce anxiety," says Rocha. In fact, studies show that consuming chocolate can reduce stress.

Dark chocolate (70% to 85% cocoa) increases levels of serotonin, a hormone linked to pleasure and well-being. With high serotonin levels, the person tends to be calmer, more relaxed.

In addition, dark chocolate acts to reduce free radicals through the antioxidants it has. "Dark chocolate is rich in flavonoids, the type of antioxidant present in cocoa. So it acts on our body in two ways: it increases serotonin levels and decreases free radicals", summarizes Rocha.

Quantity: The ideal is to eat a portion of 40 grams every day, but it must be chocolate of at least 70% cocoa. Below that, the doctor points out, chocolate will have sugar and hydrogenated fat and, therefore, will have a reverse effect. "The person will fall into the cycle that said: more blood sugar, higher glucose, and more desire to eat and anxiety."

2. Green Tea

When we talk about fighting anxiety, we basically talk about two brain neurotransmitter issues: we want to increase serotonin and increase GABA. And that is exactly how black stripe medicines work, but they have several side effects ... When GABA increases, the person sleeps better, but green tea stimulates the increase of this transmitter in a more natural way. "

Green tea also contains epigallocatechin-3-gallate (EGCG), an antioxidant that increases GABA and reduces cortisol in the body. "Cortisol can't be high in the blood and brain, and green tea helps control it. High levels of cortisol get the body inflamed and cause a variety of diseases," the doctor adds. "It [green tea] increases GABA and decreases cortisol."

Quantity: For those who like to make tea, they need to drink from 500 ml to 1 liter throughout the day. It can be taken cold or hot. Avoid industrialized sachet tea; prefer to buy the natural herb. If you are not a fan of tea, the best option is to take 1 to 2 grams capsules a day.

3. Saffron

Turmeric has in its basic principle turmeric, which plays an important role in relieving anxiety. "Turmeric has a host of antioxidants and anti-inflammatories that calm the mind, improve mental health and counteract the action of free radicals in the brain," says Patrick Rocha.

In addition, the doctor says that turmeric also decreases inflammatory markers, called cytokines, that make people agitated. "So turmeric has a natural effect on reducing anxiety as it decreases cytokines and free radicals in the brain."

Quantity: In this case, the doctor recommends the use of capsules. "It is possible to use turmeric powder to season chicken and fish, but to ensure its anti-inflammatory effects, it would need to use about 1 to 2 grams. It would be a very strong seasoning," he says, adding that, associated with black pepper, Turmeric absorption is up to 100% higher.

4. Yogurt

Taking care of mental health also involves taking care of the proper functioning of our second brain. Rich in probiotics, essential bacteria for gut health, whole natural yogurt has good fat, which in addition to food, promotes a feeling of satiety for longer.

"The gut is now considered our second brain because it produces a series of neurotransmitters that contribute to brain health and are linked to anxiety, " says Rocha. He explains:

"A healthy gut flora, that is, we are talking about a low carbohydrate diet rich in healthy protein and fat, which has many probiotics that better absorb nutrients, vitamins, and minerals, and stops absorbing toxins. We can say a lot about people's health by the bacteria in their intestinal flora. "

If you don't like yogurt, there are alternatives like curd and kefir.

Yogurt needs to be natural and whole and does not advise sweetened, light, and nonfat yogurt. "People are scared by the calories of natural yogurt, but they are healthy. What is not healthy is to remove the fat that nature brought and put a hidden sugar in industrial food, and still charge more for it", criticizes.

5. Omega 3

Found in deep and freshwater fish, omega 3 regulates levels of fundamental brain components: EPA and DHA. These components regulate the production of serotonin and dopamine - which together help keep the mind relaxed. In addition, omega 3 is a powerful anti-inflammatory.

The problem is that captive fish do not have as much omega 3 as fish from Canada, Chile, and other countries. Therefore, the doctor advises opting for a good quality supplement. "If you live near the sea and like fresh fish, eating three 200 gram portions a week is ideal," he says.

Almonds, walnuts, rustic eggs and chia also have omega 3, but in very small quantities.

Magnesium

The mineral increases GABA and helps promote a good night's sleep - essential for anxiety control. "It is not asleep inducer, but it calms the mind, and so sleep comes naturally," explains Rocha.

Amount: either chloride or nitrate, the ideal is to eat 1 to 1.5 grams per day as a supplement.

CHAPTER FOURTEEN
How anxiety affects relationships

There is plenty of information on how anxiety affects our health - mentally, emotionally, and physically. Have you considered the impact anxiety can have on the health of your relationship?

For many people, just the thought of being in a relationship can cause stress. Early on in the relationship, endless concerns may arise such as: "Does he/she really like me?", "Is this relationship seriously, and will it last?"

Anxiety is a normal emotion that, in the right amount, has the function of accelerating the search for personal growth; i.e., it does not always represent a clinical picture. Anxiety is also a necessary biological resource and a natural reaction of the body to act against real threats once the problem is addressed in advance.

What may be the causes of anxiety in affective relationships?

Falling in love can be a challenge as unexpected and uncontrollable situations arise. The more you value someone, the greater can be the sense of fear of losing the person and being hurt. Ironically, this fear often arises when you are getting exactly what you wanted when you experience the love you never had.

As two people get into a relationship, it is not only things that happen between these couples that make them anxious, but how each one perceives and feels what is happening. Sometimes we have an "inner voice" that can fuel fears of maintaining close relationships. Thoughts like, "You can't trust anyone," "He really doesn't love you," "Get out before you get hurt."

This "voice" creates an inner struggle with those close to you. In addition, these negative thoughts can dramatically decrease self-esteem, increasing distrust, creating a defensive attitude, jealousy, and anxiety. Basically, feeding negative automatic thoughts that hinder happiness and contribute to excessive worry about the relationship, rather than just enjoying it.

Cause of Relationship Anxiety

Lack of Confidence: In the Future of Relationship

By far, the most common cause of relationship anxiety is uncertainty about the future of the relationship. This anxiety can be the result of many fights, previous separations, or because of distance.

Regardless of the cause, when trust in the relationship is lost, uncertainties can cause a lot of anxiety as you become unsure or unsure of what to do with your life.

Lack of Confidence in General

Of course, a lack of trust, in general, is also a problem, after things like unfaithfulness or less serious problems like a lack of commitment to family commitments.

Trust is one of the most important parts of a relationship, and if it is lost, it is very difficult to get it back to normal.

Raised Guard All the Time

Frequent flights are a problem, but the most serious problem is not only fights that involve anger - it is also the feeling of widespread concern that you will fight again.

This worry can cause extreme anxiety because you are too afraid to do anything close to your partner because you are afraid of another fight going on at any moment.

Negativity

A relationship that is experiencing difficulties also exhibits a lot of negativity.

Even the jokes are negative, and usually, most of the words you speak are critical, and the conversation between the couple is always in an unfriendly tone.

Constant negativity and negative thoughts cause anxiety, and while it is not clear exactly how negative thoughts cause anxiety, the most obvious is that negativity distances the couple.

Manifestations of Anxiety

These are just the basic reasons for anxiety in relationships, and clearly, not the only ones, but you may already have an idea where everything is starting to become a serious problem.

People who have relationship anxiety often have the same symptoms of anxiety disorder, for example:

- Insomnia
- Muscle tension
- Depression
- Excessive sweating
- Shortness of breath and chest pain
- Heart palpitations

This anxiety is very common in other areas of your life, which is why anxiety is no longer just a relationship. Generalized anxiety disorder can simply be developed because of a troubled relationship.

How to End Relationship Anxiety

There are two main things you should ask yourself in the beginning, well before you wait for a solution to your relationship:

- Is this relationship worth saving?
- Are you willing or willing to change even if your partner does not change?

The first question is self-explanatory. Not every relationship is worth trying to save, regardless of how long you are together.

Separations are actually an important part of relationships. If you assume that the purpose of any relationship is to be with a person who always makes you happy, in any fight, you will think that the person may not be the right person for you.

The second question, however, is based on a simple truth about relationships: you can only change yourself.

Even begging your partner to change anyway, it's not up to you to change him. Your job, therefore, is to do your best to be the best partner you can be, and as open as possible, hoping to motivate your partner to change as well.

Ways to Control Relationship Anxiety

With that in mind, controlling your relationship anxiety has more to do with you than with the other person, and you can't wait for a contribution from him or her. The following strategies are effective for improving your relationship anxiety:

Exercise and other anxiety reduction strategies. First, anxiety is still anxiety, and that means effective anxiety reduction strategies can help you control how you feel. Physical activity is the easiest strategy to integrate into your life right now. There is a lot of research and evidence that exercise is as powerful as most anxiety medications and anxiety symptoms control.

Start over. If trust is lost, talk to your partner about starting over and dating as you have never related before. Trust is a matter of building a foundation, and it needs to grow from scratch. However, you must always follow this plan. If, after a few weeks, things get better, it is still too early to say that confidence is restored. You will not want to fall into old habits.

Exchanging needs. Talk to your partner about their needs. Write down these needs on paper, so they both know what they want. After that, try your best to do everything your partner wants, as long as it doesn't hurt your morale. Don't expect him or her to do anything or everything on the list, just give him or her what was asked and be the best spouse you can be. You will see more motivation on the part of the other person to do so. But if it doesn't happen after a month or so, he or she probably won't want to do it later.

Keep busy mentally. Occupying the head is a proven strategy of improving the mood in the relationship. Generally, you find that your mind is your enemy in relationships, as you can imagine a multitude of things that most often do not match reality. So keep your mind away from relationships as much as possible, with activities outside the home, working more, learn new things and so on. This diminishes the power of your mind to produce negative emotions.

Give more affection. Touching, hugging, or holding your hand, even in anger at the other person, has an incredible effect. This is one of the reasons that contribute to success in the relationship. Try to stay more in physical contact for a while, even being angry with him or her.

CHAPTER FIFTEEN
Emotional Abuse And Anxiety: How Do They Relate?

Not all abuses are physical. There is another type of abuse that is also very common: the emotional one. Emotional abuse and anxiety have a significant relationship, as the latter is a common consequence that appears in people who have been in abusive relationships.

This type of abuse has serious and significant consequences for the person suffering from it. We will look at how emotional abuse and anxiety-related, and the effects they can cause without us realizing it.

What is emotional abuse?

Emotional abuse is the term used to define behaviors that a partner uses to hurt, control, manipulate, or frighten his partner.

Emotional abuse is an abuse against one's emotions rather than one's physical. However, there are more subtle forms of emotional abuse that can happen in relationships. This makes it hard to see when it happens.

Some clearer forms of emotional abuse are, for example:

- Suicide threat if you want to break up or do something your partner doesn't want you to do;

- Frequent insults, humiliations, and statements about you that hurt you;
- Control of their behaviors, including their appearance;
- Control your friends and what you can do;
- Intimidating threats or behaviors;
- Manipulation of behaviors.

Other much more subtle ways of emotionally abusing other people are as follows:

- The "silent treatments," where one refuses to talk to anyone;
- Refusal of sex to get something;
- Negative jokes with no purpose or attempt to propel the partner;
- Threatening to leave the relationship (or leaving home) after an argument ;
- Do not allow the partner to talk to anyone of the opposite sex;
- Check partner phone for calls, messages, etc .;
- Demonstrate jealous often, even without reason;
- Blame your partner for things that are not working out with yourself.

Clearly, few people can say they have not emotionally abused their partners (or their children, parents, or others) at any time. But if these behaviors happen frequently and affect the way you or your partner think, feel, or act, you may find yourself in an emotionally abusive relationship.

Emotional Abuse and Anxiety: Effects of Unseen Abuse

Emotional abuse may not cause any physical bruising or put the person at risk of serious physical injury. However, the effects of emotionally abusive relationships are relevant and can have lasting emotional consequences.

People who live in an emotionally abusive relationship may feel they are worthless, as their relationship can erode their self-esteem and confidence. They may also become sad or depressed and may even feel pain for no apparent reason. In addition, they may feel alone or feel alone if their partner leaves them.

However, not everyone has these symptoms. All the people are different. For example, because emotional abuse may be bilateral (i.e., both emotionally abusive), it is also likely that the same behaviors will happen on both sides: anger, silent treatment, or screaming, among others.

There is also a symptom that tends to spread out of the relationship that can last a lifetime if left untreated: anxiety. In fact, anxiety is perhaps one of the most common symptoms of emotional abuse.

Sometimes anxiety is limited to the relationship; in others, it can spread to various situations, such as at work, for example. It may also remain after the relationship ends.

Emotional abuse often causes anxiety as it is virtually a storm of anxiety-provoking events:

Creates chronic stress, which is one of the most common causes of anxiety;

- Causes excessive thinking;
- It leads to low self-esteem and self-confidence;
- It makes people feel nervous and worried that others might hurt them.
- It nullifies social support as it is caused by someone they need to have support.

This combination of different problems makes emotional abuse easily trigger anxiety symptoms in those who experience it in the short and long term. In more severe cases, it can lead to a combination of anxiety and depression or even panic attacks.

CHAPTER SIXTEEN
Anxiety at work: How the disorder interferes with working life

In general, any anxiety problem is distressing, but when these problems affect the workplace, they can be even more so. In the current times, where anxiety problems are becoming more common, the work environment is no exception, especially if it fits with the panorama of instability and crisis experienced in recent years.

However, anxiety problems often have nothing to do with the objective context. You may even do well objectively in your work and may suffer from many worries, fears, and anxiety in your work activity.

How does anxiety occur at work?

Job anxiety does not come from anywhere. There are various causes that cause and trigger this situation. There are several factors that can cause this anxiety response at work. Among them, the most common are:

Negative anticipation (Catastrophism): This factor occurs when we receive a new task or that we do not master. It may happen that we get to interpret that we will not be able to do it. We may even imagine that our boss will not like it and that it will have catastrophic consequences. In such cases, we are alarmed, and that state of anxiety begins to occur, caused by that fear of new work.

High labor demand: If we tend to offer ourselves to the most complicated tasks and are very perfectionist with our work, it is easy to fall into a state of anxiety. This type of situation of labor self-demand keeps us tense and with a feeling of continuous stress. This environment can cause anxiety in the work we are talking about.

The tendency to control: Not all work can be under our control. Wanting to cover every task and every responsibility is a mistake. If we overload our time with tasks that do not belong to us, we will enter into a state of anxiety about work. Teamwork and the possibility of delegating exist so that all the weight does not fall on a single person. Remember it.

Fear of making mistakes: Fear of mistakes is another of the main reasons for anxiety at work. Not valuing mistakes as good patterns to evolve, and as a reason to torture, causes that state commonly known as work depression.

Fear of negative evaluation: Sometimes, an evaluation that is not positive, can create doubts in us. If criticism affects us even more, those doubts translate to fear. And that fear ends up producing a state of anxiety at work. Assimilating all kinds of assessments to grow work and personally, will help dissipate that stress.

What are the symptoms of anxiety at work?

Now what reasons usually because of anxiety at work, we will identify it. And it is that this state of stress and anxiety becomes visible in us in different ways:

Tense muscles

Depending on how we react to our work demands, it will result in muscle tension. This stress overload when performing tasks leads to contractures and muscle discomfort. They are quite frequent in many jobs. If they occur continuously, it is one of the symptoms of this anxiety at work.

Obsession for perfectionism

The state of anxiety and stress produced can lead to obsessing for perfection in our activities. To think that only with that perfection will we obtain greater security and tranquillity, it will only lead us to stress more. It is another of the symptoms with which that anxiety is better appreciated at work.

Personal insecurity

It is derived from this obsession with perfectionism. Not being able to meet all these high demands, a negative self-assessment is produced. Seeing us as incapable or unproductive causes constant personal insecurity that becomes visible in states of anxiety.

Job insecurity

Being constantly suspicious of a possible loss of the job is another symptom of anxiety at work. Despite having positive feedback from our company, we can feel that insecurity. See constantly jeopardize the post, generates greater stress and anxiety.

Eating disorder

Anxiety is noticeable in other personal habits. Faced with high levels of stress, many people tend to calm down by eating unhealthy foods. It is another consequence and at the same time, symptoms of anxiety at work.

Insomnia

In anxiety states caused by work, the body remains alert even at night. Sometimes, we are reviewing all tasks and activities to try to make them perfect. Thinking 24 hours a day in our employment, leads to strong stress situations.

Consequences of anxiety at work

Anxiety at work causes a series of consequences in us. We do not speak only of anguish to go to work, but of many other consequences. The most notorious are:

Tiredness or exhaustion: With such demand and concern, any work becomes arduous and tedious. A constant state of tension results in noticeable and palpable exhaustion.

Excessive concern: If we are in a state of anxiety at work, we will feel constant concern. Good for self-demand, for that absolute perfectionism, or for fear of being valued negatively.

Maintenance of anxiety: Time passes, we change workloads, including bosses and jobs, but we remain equally stressed. It is another of the great consequences of anxiety at work.

Excessive verification of tasks: The obsession with perfectionism and the fear of making mistakes makes us constantly review everything. Adding that review to our already busy schedule creates even more anxiety and stress.

Slowness: The constant review of tasks delays our pace more. This slow feedback feeds our state of anxiety since we have time to complete the rest of the activities. Thus we reach a point of greater stress that does not cease.

Do not disconnect: Due to all the factors mentioned above, we will be constantly attentive to the tasks entrusted to us. In addition, we will be waiting to respond as soon as possible to any demand.

Prevent anxiety at work

We already know what anxiety is at work. We know the main factors that cause it and its consequences. But, an important issue knows what to do to calm anxiety. Here are some tips to overcome anxiety:

Organize your time calmly

It is important to devote time to all areas of our life. Do not let the labor part absorb leisure, social life, etc ... Therefore, we have to reasonably distribute time for all areas of our life. Only then will we avoid focusing all our energies on one thing.

Perform physical exercise

Exercise helps us to have good physical and mental health. It also helps us to disconnect from work. Through the practice of sport, we place limits on the part of our life that occupies employment. We will also clear our responsibilities, thus avoiding that anxiety at work.

Ask an expert for help

When we see that our emotional state begins to be overwhelming both in the work and personal environment, it would be convenient to consult with a psychologist. An anxiety specialist can assess our case and establish an appropriate therapy. It is another of the great ways to overcome anxiety at work.

Request work leave due to anxiety at work

If you think you have anxiety at work and need leave from work, you should see a Social Security doctor. They will analyze your situation, diagnosing, and assessing whether a work leave is necessary or not.

CONCLUSION

Human beings are social beings; we have lived in society for millions of years. This way of life has defined our way of relating to others. Everything we do in our lives has a social component.

The importance of this social component is such that there is a widespread belief that people with more sympathy and more social appeal are more valued. And it is also believed that this social appeal is innate, and we can do nothing to change it. This is not totally true. There is an innate component, but reality tells us that sympathy, the ability to relate to others is something that is acquired through experience.

Since we are young and we begin to interact with others, and that happens from the moment of birth, gradually, the relationships in our lives are modeled; little by little, the experience with others is teaching us how to behave in certain situations.

Therefore, we can say that skills are acquired through learning, first in the family, and then extended to the rest of society. Just as we learn to speak, to walk, we still learn to relate, and the skills necessary for it.

Made in the USA
Las Vegas, NV
26 March 2022